Cyberattack!

*A nightmare journey into the world of
the digital unknown*

@GlobalWork collection – Part II

Original text by Angeline Vagabulle

Illustrations by Renard

Preface by General Marc Watin-Augouard

English translation by Andrew Baggaley

For the latest news about the #GlobalWorkCollection, you can find us on Facebook here:
https://www.facebook.com/GlobalWorkCollection/

You can also find Angeline Vagabulle on FaceZinZin, LinkGlouGlou, InstaBlurk and Twitbird @vagabulle as well as the author's website:
http://angelinevagabulle.wixsite.com/angelinevagabulle

Thalia NeoMedia / DG Editions Les Funambulles

The English translation of this book has been made possible thanks to the support of the following sponsors :

- *Atelier Arts et Lettres, www.atelierartsetlettres.fr*
- *Philippe Aurain*
- *Florence Barnaud, author, « Sangs Eternels »*
- *Marie-Noëlle Borel, Institut des Sciences de la Personnalité www.institut-sciences-perso.fr*
- *Melody Burton, consultant*
- *Bertrand Bussière*
- *Christophe Chambet-Falquet*
- *Michèle Côme, ComeInc Humour Incorporated, www.comeinc.fr*
- *Mauro Cossu*
- *Ed Arty, author, "Le Conseil ou la Vie"*
- *Effective Yellow: Frédéric Vilanova et Christophe Clarinard*
- *Adeline Desthuilliers*
- *Nathalie Dupuis-Hepner*
- *Sophie Floreani, writer, www.ara-and-co.com, ARA&CO*
- *Lindsay Gerrand*
- *Jean-Michel Guibert*
- *Estelle Guillerm, CaféZen and FamilyZen founder*
- *Laurent Marchal*
- *Sandra Thevenaz*
- *Maurice Tixier*
- *S. van Gilst*

For the hyperconnected Erwan, Benjamin & Maël,

For Rébecca, who helped me discover WhatsApp,

For Jean-Michel, the most beautiful connection in my life,

Preface

Authors are inspired by current affairs, and that's why more and more books are being published on the subject of cyberspace. While the digital revolution has allowed us to dream about a future filled with hope, the threat of cyberattacks are also of equal fascination as we become aware that any one of us could become the victim of digital crime, throwing them into a world of virtual conflict. Both individuals and companies alike are finding themselves in the middle of a planet-wide firing line, invisible cyberweapons pointed right at them, all the while believing they are being aimed at somebody else.

Reading books on these subjects is often an unpleasant experience. The first few pages are typically filled with technical jargon, which is designed to let the reader know that this author knows what they're talking about. The more obscure the language, the more the subject matter must appear to the neophyte and the more the author distances themselves from the average reader, positioning themselves as one of the rare savants to hold the keys to the knowledge vault. Add a pinch of sensationalism, talk a little about a cyber war wherever possible, and the work serves as a vehicle to placing the author as one of the privileged « experts » in the field who generously share their opinions on TV shows and in newspapers.

Mercifully, there are exceptions. Often discreet, hidden behind the books where the reputation of the author or a "communication plan" has managed to secure the pride of place upon the shelf, are these hidden gems. Those books that make bibliophiles purr when they get their hands on one of these rare pearls.

I was fortunate to experience this type of joy for myself, thanks to "Cyberattack!". Even the name of the author brought a kind of poetry to a subject that can seem daunting. Perhaps it was the illustrations that made me decide to give the book a fair chance. If a good sketch is able to reinforce words, I certainly appreciate having an artists' view of a digital space that is inherently immaterial.

When I see the date of June 27, 2017, I am immediately reminded of what happened with 'NotPetya' virus, one of the most serious attacks in the (ongoing!) history of cybercrime. Finally, I was going to know everything, in detail, about this devastating attack. But from the outset, I realized that this was not going to be a forensic technical analysis of what happened, or at least not totally. It's easy to understand language that Angeline Vagabulle guided me towards the essential truth: the place of the human being in this digital revolution.

Angeline's talent is reflected in her art of recounting this tale. Through little touches intelligently integrated into the story, she is able to teach us lessons by using real examples that she experienced, creating a book where "fiction meets reality".

This book is a deeply human one, because it shows us how weak we are in our loneliness when we are "disconnected". Two other authors have already written about the "age of the multitude" that seems to be occurring with this digital revolution. A multitude of hyperconnected Internet users, 'communitized' through social networks, freed from the constraints of space and time. Suddenly, in a company that has been hit hard by cybercrime, it's precisely the isolation of these same individuals that is the first manifestation of the cyberattack. All links are cut off, memory is lost or overwritten.

It's true that loneliness and silence are the first symptoms of an illness that is thought to be benign, the effects of which will not last. Just a bad period that will eventually pass. But very quickly the reality becomes more painful. The illusion of being in a network vanishes. It is a veritable catastrophe, if we are judging by the loss of data and turnover, or by the damage done to a reputation. But while we accompany our heroine through her daily life, we also discover that the cyberattack has positive consequences: it teaches us to behave like human beings, to talk to our colleagues, to find the sense of the collective, to reinvent the means that we use to communicate. Of course, it is easy to say that bad is worse than good and that it's possible to make these realizations without being the victims of a cyberattack. That may be true, but no one seems to do anything about this situation when everything is going well. Only adversity puts us in the right condition to put ourselves back into our human condition.

Reading this book felt like a friend was telling me a story, a friend whose company had recently been "neutralized" for a month. Victims of NotPetya or other such treacherous attacks (Wannacry, for example) on other companies, large or small, will recognize themselves in this tale.

There's a moral to every story. In this case, it lies in the imperative need to rethink our organizations during this digital revolution. While organizations should free us, they can also make us slaves if their way of working makes us too dependent on digital tools. But the main moral, Angeline gives us by inviting us to reconnect to our "fundamentals of life". It does not question the rise of digital technologies but relativizes their importance.

We have forgotten what it means to be human and abandoned our true nature; but after a cyberattack, it comes back with a bang!

In the age of "everything digital", the paperback is still doing well, and this is not the only unexpected survivor. It's good news for those who like to feel, see and smell the paper in order to truly 'read' something. Whatever format you have chosen, I hope you enjoy your reading of "Cyberattack!".

General Marc Watin-Augouard
Director of the EOGN Research Centre (CREOGN)
Founder and co-director of the International Cybersecurity Forum (FIC)

It's now been a few months now since I decided to start documenting all of the humorous happenings at the large multinational organization where I work. In a previous book[1,] I described some of my experiences working in La Défense, France's primary business district, and my business trips to the four corners of the world wearing my big colorful coat. After a few years of working in that high-pressure environment, I began to get quite tired of the lifestyle. I was constantly jetting off to some new and distant horizon, and frankly, it was exhausting. Around this time, my company decided that they were going to send me to Strasbourg, a much smaller French city on the border with Germany. I'd been assigned to go work there for a few months. It would be goodbye to the skyscrapers and gray paving slabs of La Défense, and hello to what I thought would be a more serene and peaceful way of life. It promised to be a little less alienating than Paris and I'd be working in an office that was a little more reasonably sized.

Of course, nothing happens as it is supposed to. In this world of overconfident multinational organizations, an event that was as unexpected as it was unlikely would occur during my time there. My peaceful little sojourn would take a turn that would remind me just how fragile our world really is, and that this gigantic company is

---

[1] Global Work: It's a Topsy-Turvy World!

nothing more than a giant with feet of clay. I'd made sure to pack my sense of humor, and it turned out to be a very wise decision. I'd need it to deal with the smorgasbord of emotions that I would have to endure on a regular basis as the company descended into absolute chaos.

My Alsatian adventure brought me face to face with the realities of our relationship with technology, especially in the world of work, where it could be accurately described as an addiction. The majority of the events described in this book actually happened. Most of the conversations are faithful retellings, with a little cosmetic work here and there to ensure the protagonists are not easily identified.

A long time ago, in a large multinational corporation, far, far away ...

If there's one word that perfectly describes multinational corporations, it's *hyperconnected*. The vast majority of the work that they engage in (read: all of it) can only be done if the IT network is in perfect working order.

It's a change that's happened over the last twenty years, at something approaching the speed of light. Many people have witnessed this (r)evolution right from its very beginnings.

It's a little difficult to remember how it was before, although I should like to point out here that I am not a frail old lady just yet. And I say that with the utmost respect for our elders. It is a fact, however, that emails did not exist twenty years ago. Nor smartphones or video conferences. When I started working for a big consultancy firm toward the beginning of my career, we didn't have laptops and the desktop computers were incredibly sluggish and not very user friendly, to say the least. The rickety old word processors used to record the minutes of meetings had all been put into storage by that point, but we still weren't exactly firing out PowerPoint presentations or crafting complex pivot tables just yet, either. Conversations took place during meetings where actual people were present, while conference calls were still very much a rarity. We printed sheets of paper with notes on to bring into meetings.

Our agendas were also made of paper. I remember fondly my very first Palm Pilot, an electronic device that allowed the user to store their agenda and contacts in one place. You could even connect it to the computer to 'sync' all of your info on both devices. You were supposed to do this twice a day. Once in the morning when you arrived and once just before you left.

We even had one-hour lunchbreaks. Colleagues ate together and conversed about everything and nothing. Each Friday afternoon, we gathered with our fellow co-workers to share a drink and engage in some light conversation about how our week had gone. Working with colleagues from an office in another city only happened exceptionally rarely. I sometimes worked with our colleagues in Lyon. We very occasionally sent each other documents by fax to prepare for client meetings.

And then, suddenly, everything changed.

Now, a typical workday in the spring of 2017, goes something a little more like this...

Research from PWC estimates that there are 177,300 cyberattacks per day throughout the world.

In 2014 alone, the number of hacking incidents increased by 48%. Since 2009, they have increased by an average of 66% per year.

Cybersecurity Ventures predicted that the annual cost of cybercrime will cost the world $6 trillion annually by 2021, up from $3 trillion in 2015. This represents the greatest transfer of economic wealth in history.

Everything was going smoothly on this Monday morning, just as it always tends to do at large companies like mine. I had a typical day lined up. My calendar was full of meetings and conference calls; one right after the other.

I'd only just woken up when I looked at my agenda for the first time, sitting on the end of my bed holding my smartphone. While I was sleeping, a colleague in Asia had scheduled me to be in a call with the Middle East at 1.30 pm. That meant that today, I would only have 30 minutes when I was not on some call or another. This oasis of time was easy to spot on my agenda, as it was the only part of my day not colored in dark blue. I'd would have to have lunch 'al desk-o' during my 12 pm – 1 pm call. That's fine – I'll just have to put the microphone on silent so the other callers can't hear me chewing. So, a very typical day, all in all. It will no doubt be the same tomorrow and the day after that.

The day began with my regular monthly call to a manager in Sydney. After that, there was the project I was working on with three colleagues who were all based abroad; one in Dubai, one in London and the other in Frankfurt. Once that was finished, the rest of my day would be a surprise. In any case, I wouldn't have any time to prepare for what came next anyway. Right now the priority was getting to the office on time. A quick shower, throw on some clothes, breakfast while standing, say bye to the kids and close the door behind me.

I use my time on the train to scan through the 26 emails that I've received during the night.

I'm reminded of various important tasks that need to be completed during the day ahead. I have no idea how I'm supposed to do that with all of these conference calls, however. I won't even have enough time to breathe, let alone grab a coffee, think (which can be useful at work) or even use the bathroom. I start working before I even arrive, sending a few messages. It's how it's always been and how it will always be. We spend our days chasing time and objectives.

As I arrive, I can feel the stress hormones pumping through my body already. It's 8.25 am. I have 5 minutes before I'm supposed to be at my desk, plugged into my computer. Just enough time to grab a coffee. I say an almost-hello to the receptionist with a vague gesture. There's no one else here. No one in the elevators; no one in the corridors. It's still early. Most people on my floor start a bit later. I hardly know anyone, having just arrived a few days ago for my new temporary role. I've had a few brief conversations here and there when the undulating rhythm of the workflow in the international corporation allows me to. I say a very quick 'hi' to the cleaning lady who's about to finish her shift. Sometimes, when I arrive early, I like to talk with her for a while before I begin my day. Not today though. No time for that!

The 8.30 call goes well. Apparently it was very cold in Sydney. Next, a conference call about a project. It's still hot in Dubai, raining in London and positively miserable in Frankfurt. How was the weather in Strasbourg? No idea. I was too busy looking at my smartphone.

I logon to the company network before my next meeting starts to validate an invoice that needs to be paid. The meeting that follows has been organized to help us prepare for the launch of a new product with the marketing team. We're joined on the call by the Paris, Amsterdam, Rome and Leeds offices. By some miracle we finish a few minutes early and I can't believe my luck. I have ten long, precious minutes all to myself before the next meeting begins at 1 pm. I make a beeline for the restrooms before heading back to my desk to catch up on the news. I munch mindlessly on a sandwich that I bought from a machine between my 10 o'clock call and 11 o'clock calls.

1.45 pm: The next meeting ended later than planned (some people still hadn't connected by 1 pm so we started late), so now I only have 15 minutes to finish everything. As I head towards my desk, I read the dozen or so messages that I labeled 'urgent' on my phone on my way to work. It's a bit difficult to find them now though, as I've received another 40 in the meantime. A few of those are replies to the emails that I was looking for, but now with added information, including various attachments. I read a document (diagonally) about a budget, as well as an executive report. I don't have time to finish it now, so I'll print it to read on the way home. I write a few replies to some priority emails and write around fifteen more of my own. I also use the opportunity to work on a message that I'll be sending to members of my own team a little later in the week.

2 pm: I join the meeting. I'm the only person online. A few minutes later, still no one.

Strange. I check my mails. Whaddya know! The meeting was canceled at 1.58 pm by the project manager:

'Due to the number of people saying they cannot attend at the last minute, I am canceling the 2 pm meeting.'

It's probably for the best. Now I can prepare for my trip to the States next month. I need to complete a flight reservation form online then send it to the online travel agency. The e-ticket will be sent to me by email by the end of next week.

3 pm: Meeting about the rollout of a new system that will allow us to upload information about our clients that all employees will be able to access online. The rollout will be global, so all of the regional managers, as well as the central project team based in Madrid, are in the meeting.

Suddenly a chat window opens on my screen. It's one of my colleagues in Stockholm letting me know that there's a problem with a file. It would appear that the Warsaw team are running late with a report that's supposed to be delivered that evening to a client. I call Warsaw. It's considered to be a serious enough situation for us all to connect with our webcams. Calls tend to go better when we can actually see each other. The team seems tired. I try to give them a morale boost. We agree that it's very important to respect the deadline for this very important client, so we all figure out a way to catch up with the work that needs to be done.

6 pm: Crap! While I was dealing with the crisis in Warsaw, I missed a conference call with a colleague in Amsterdam who wanted to discuss a CV for a job hire. I also missed a call with our management accountant to discuss the budget preparations for next year. My screen is lighting up with chat boxes and messages from people who are trying to get hold of me.

Suddenly I feel an enormous wave of exhaustion. It must nearly be time for me to go home. And thanks to my smartphone, I'll be able to read all my messages on the train during on my way. I can even write to my colleague in Amsterdam and the people in finance whom I ghosted. It would be perfect if we could find a time to talk before the end of the week, but with the way my agenda is looking, I don't think that's going to be easy.

I'm on the train looking through the messages on my phone. I've received 250 emails today. Thirty are automated, and the rest are pretty much pointless. This assignment in Strasbourg hasn't really given me much time to get to know my colleagues.

One of the emails is from our IT director, Dominic. His long, rambling messages always make me laugh a little. Most of the time I just skim through them, because more often than not, I don't understand a thing he writes. They're ridiculously overblown and complicated, but written as if it were aimed at his kids.

Subject: WannaCry.

Wannacry wannacry, we will really cry?

Ok, what are you trying to tell us, Dominic ?

Definition

A cyberattack is a malicious act against a computer device through a cybernetic network. Cyberattacks can be executed by individuals (Kevin Mitnick, for example, one of the most notorious), a small group of pirates (or hackers), or more recently by large organizations with geopolitical objectives.

Dominic's message in full:
E-mail

****

From: Dominic Invulnerable
To: All
Subject: WannaCry

I'm sure you've all heard the news recently about the ransomware Wannacry. This pernicious virus has already spread to over 70 countries, affecting many large organizations over the last 24 hours. Our global IT team has carefully evaluated our environment and we can confirm that, thus far, we have not been infected and should not be affected going forward.

This is not enough, however. We will take preventative measures to protect the network over the weekend, and from 6 pm Saturday many online services will be unavailable for a period of two hours.

The protective system of our information environment plays a vital role in defending against cyberattacks, but YOU also play a key role in our defense. Please be extremely vigilant, especially when asked to click on any links received by email. If you are unsure about the authenticity of an email, do not click on any links contained within it. If you notice anything suspect or abnormal on your computer at any moment, please let us know immediately.

Dominic Invulnerable
Chief Information Officer
****

Alright. Got it. No need to be so dramatic. I reschedule a few of my meetings in my online agenda. I take a quick look at what I've got coming up tomorrow. It's more or less the same as what I had today. Except for the video interview I have for a job that we're recruiting for in Germany. It'll make a change from all of my conference calls. Anyway, time to log off. My train has arrived.

I turn off my phone.

The incessant stream of messages slips into obscurity with the slow sigh of the soon-to-be sleeping device.

The threat that this virus truly poses may be over our heads, but there are definitely storm clouds gathering over the IT system.

I'm on the train for my usual daily commute to the office. Time to send a few messages. I'll also use this time to begin the annual report that I need to send to our directors before the end of the month.

The incessant stream of messages begins again after the slow sigh from the soon-to-be restarted device. Before I start writing, I take a look at what I missed while I was sleeping. A dozen messages from Asia Pacific about the launch of the new system. I'll talk about it when I arrive at the office with my manager who's based in Hong Kong. We have a call scheduled for 9 am.

Wait, what's this? Another email from our CIO! This guy doesn't let up. His message seems a little odd though. Feels like I'd better read it, properly. I take a deep breath. Brevity isn't exactly Dominic's strong point.

Considered to be the single biggest ransomware attack in history, in just a few hours WannaCry has infected more than 300,000 computers in over 150 countries. Its victims include FedEx, Renault and even the Russian Interior Ministry.

The hacker group 'Shadow Brokers' has claimed responsibility for the attack. This is the same group who, in early 2017, managed to break into the network of the NSA, plundering a not-inconsiderable amount of loot including viruses and various other IT tools and exploits. One of these was used for the WannaCry attack, codenamed EternalBlue. Microsoft was seemingly aware of the exploits, but the patch they issued was not installed on a large enough scale for it to be effective in protecting against the intrusion.

Ultimately, the eventual cost of the WannaCry cryptoworm is estimated to be in the region of one billion dollars, and that is of course without counting the possible indirect consequences that may affect victims.

$1,000,000,000
WANNACRY

E-mail

****

From: Dominic Invulnerable
To: All

Subject: WannaCry

I have some new information to share with you following my previous message, which I have left copied below (read that one first).

Our evaluation of the situation remains as I previously described in my first message. We must wait to see how the epidemic spreads and what effects it will have once we return to work next week, but fortunately for the moment, at the time of writing, we remain unaffected and are continuing to evaluate the multiple levels of security we have installed in order to ensure that they are able to maintain the situation as it currently stands.

As part of the precautionary measures that we are obliged to take, we plan to restart all company computers (laptops included) when you arrive on Monday morning and connect to the network. If you are not in the office on Monday, it will be done at the first opportunity after that. This will ensure that all computers have the necessary security updates installed. You may see a window appear on your computer screen explaining that the update is taking place or asking you to confirm shutting down your computer. Please do not delay this update from taking place. Click on 'Accept' and let the installation commence. If you do not see a dialogue window, or if your computer does not restart, please do not worry. We assure you that all necessary steps to protect your computer will be undertaken. We will also be performing a forced reboot of all computers Monday evening.

I emphasize once again that YOU also play a key role in the security and protection of the company's network. Please make sure that your computer does indeed reboot, and once it does, let us know if anything that looks strange or suspicious happens. Please stay vigilant with your emails. Do not click on any links contained within an email unless you are absolutely sure about its authenticity.

Your CIO,
Dominic Invulnerable
****

I'm really not sure about all this.

Our dear Dominic seems kinda panicky. I think I'll do a little web investigation on this virus thing.

The beginning on the 1990s is the period of time mostly associated with the emergence of cybernetic crime, commonly known as hacking. The first nationwide crackdown against such activity was Operation Sundevil in 1990. The emergence of cyberspace also accelerated the democratization of cracking, phreaking and hacking techniques.

I don't know what any of that means.

Cracking: Pretty sure that's something to do with cocaine.

Phreaking: They're a creative bunch these IT guys. But this is a bit terrifying. Makes me think of circus freaks.

Hacking: Yep, of course. I know this one. When someone harpoons your account like a pirate then rummages around your private quarters looking for treasure.

Ugh.

So anyway, 'cracking', at least in an IT sense, is the act gaining or attempting to gain unauthorized access into a computer network in order to tamper with systems, programs or databases.

The word 'phreaking' is obtained by combining the words 'phone' and 'freak.' People who are involved in telephonic piracy are known as 'phreakers.'

Phreakers may use a phone operator's network in order to access to special functions, such as getting free calls and/or for anonymity.

In certain countries this is, of course, illegal. However, certain phreakers adamantly claim that they have no nefarious aims and are simply investigating the technology in order to learn new techniques.

Hacking is the word the public usually associates with the activities performed by crackers, that is to say computer crime. While this may be the most common usage, hackers deny that it is the correct term, claiming that they are merely computer enthusiasts with advanced-level knowledge in coding and computer systems.

Hmm. I have to admit, it's a little worrying to know that there are people, some well-intentioned, others not-so-much, floating around in cyberspace who could gain access to my private information at any given moment, should they so desire.

Sure of its own invincibility, the Titanic carved through the seas full steam ahead, right for the iceberg...

Somehow, the week was already coming to an end. It was Friday. Or 'Happy Friday', as my English colleagues like to call it. At last! Two days all to myself. I needed the break. I didn't know what time it was, where I lived or what language I spoke anymore, after all of these international conference calls with people at the other end of the planet for five days without pause.

8 pm. I glance at my phone robotically so I can read just one more message before turning it off. Bring on the weekend. I read the message and I disconnect. Completely. I promise.

Wait, there's another message from Dominic...

E-mail

****

From: Dominic Invulnerable
To: All
Subject : End of week message

Although it's nearing the end of the week, I'd like to take the opportunity to once again assure you that the company has not been affected by the virus.

I'd also like to thank you all for your understanding during the inconvenience caused this week, including the forced rebooting of your computers and the automatic shutdown that occurred in the evening.

I'd just like to remind you to remain vigilant for anything that might seem out of the ordinary, including emails of unknown origin that contain links, websites that may seem untrustworthy, or a memory card that you don't remember having seen before. We are still uncertain as to the origins of the WannaCry virus. It is possible that it was a phishing campaign, a website that had been compromised, or the virus was directly planted somewhere.

Don't forget to protect your personal devices at home either. Keep your antivirus software updated, download any available system updates and be wary of any suspicious links sent to you (you should in fact be more wary at home than

you are in the workplace as we have strict measures
in place to protect you from a lot of possible
problems).

Your CIO,
Dominic Invulnerable

****

Yeah, now I'm really starting to worry.

There's something about him that doesn't seem entirely convincing. You can see the sweat seeping from between the lines of his message, despite his calm and paternal tone that's still just as irritating as ever. I wouldn't like to be in his shoes right now. It seems like he's getting ready for something to hit the fan. The only thing he's not sure of is when it's going to happen.

He didn't write this message to reassure me.

But now he's got me worrying about what could happen in my own home, on MY computer. What's really going on here?

It's time to turn off my phone and think about something else. I'm just happy that I don't work in IT. This time my phone is off *for good*. It's weighing me down. It's 8.15 pm.

*And somehow, despite all of his attempts to
protect us and his reassuring messages, we too
would soon wanna cry.*

The first cyberattack targeting a nation's government took place in 2007. The attack lasted a few weeks. Those responsible flooded government websites with so much traffic that they were effectively rendered totally unusable for a not-inconsequential period of time. The source of the attacks was discovered to be Russia. The bandits targeted the Estonian government's administrative websites, as well as banks and newspapers.

The Estonian government had for a few years used a non-paper based policy for its administrative activities, relying instead on multiple digital locations to store and manage its information. All of their websites and other digitally-stored data were linked via the servers they were stored upon. This type of 'non-paper' set-up left the country particularly vulnerable to an attack of this nature.

Although it was the first known cyberattack of its kind and rather simple in its execution, it had been extremely effective. Simply connect as many times as possible to the same network and shut it down through the sheer volume of traffic. This method has since become a favorite method for hackers, mainly due to its discretion. One person controls multiple computers and remains lost among the flood of IP addresses. The combined onslaught of connections controlled by the hacker is what's known as a 'botnet'.

The days continued to fly by at the same rapid pace for the rest of June. An endless flow of projects, business trips and virtual conference calls. Documents were being sent, edited and sent back with more people involved each time. Day after day the servers had more information to process.

Everyone was working their hardest to make sure the large multinational corporation kept going strong, no matter what.

D-Day.

That's weird. When I try to open this Excel file, a strange message pops up. Why doesn't it recognize the extension? What do you mean the file is corrupt?

I open up the online chat with the IT helpdesk.

'Hello?'
'..........................*Please wait. We are searching for an available agent..............*'
Two minutes later:
'*We're sorry, there are no agents available at the moment. Please try again later.*'
Ten minutes later:
'Hello. I have an issue with an Excel spreadsheet. Can you help?'
'..........................*Please wait. We are searching for an available agent..............*'
Two minutes later:
'*We're sorry, there are no agents available at the moment. Please try again later.*'

OK, I'll have to solve this later it seems. I need to finish up the presentation to send to my German colleague for the meeting in Holland tomorrow afternoon. The brief is scheduled for 1.30 pm.

1.22 pm: A little message pops into my inbox: 'We have been the victim of a cyberattack. Shut down your computers.'

1.23 pm: I shut my computer down, as instructed.

No more computer means no more communication. That includes the thing that we used to call a 'telephone', which also won't work anymore because it all goes through the computer these days. I'll have to use my cellphone for the 1.30 pm call.

I check my emails on my phone. There's another mail from IT that says something like 'Whatever you do, don't shut down your computers!' I should have known. Well, too late. Mine's already off.

There are shuffling noises coming from the corridors. People are actually getting up and leaving their offices. I realize that I have lots of colleagues that I've never even seen before. Maybe we should shut down our computers a little more often! It would make meeting people a lot easier. Rather than spending the majority of my day chatting with people on the other side of the world, I could actually cultivate some real-life relationships with the people who work on the same corridor as I do.

It didn't take long for everything to come to a halt. I personally couldn't do anything without my computer. At all. It had been a while since they'd taken my landline telephone away (I find myself staring enviously at the one on the desk of an accountant nearby). I use my cellphone to make a call to a colleague in the Middle East. Apparently they have exactly the same problem and she too is only able to communicate by using her cellphone.

I call my colleague in England. We were supposed to have a video conference about a job hire later that afternoon. It seemed like we could still do video conferences after all. Unfortunately, he'd forgotten to make the request online, and now that we could no longer send any emails (the horror), it's highly unlikely that our friends in IT will be able to set up the call.

I call my colleague in Germany. He's having the same issues. The presentation tomorrow is going to be tough. It's saved on my computer, which I can't switch on. I can't send anything because I have no email. He can't receive anything anyway because he has no computer and no email. This is all probably going to blow over soon enough. Everything will be back to normal before we leave this evening, I'm positive. I mean, it has to be. I'll just wake up earlier than usual tomorrow to finish the presentation and send it to Karl-Hans.

This is all reminding me of the commercials for constipation medication. Just swallow one big pill and everything will loosen up and we'll be able to get right back to work.

My German colleague suggests that I just send him the presentation to his personal email address. Great idea, but that would mean redoing the entire presentation on my computer at home this evening. Plus I don't have all of the tools that I'd need, like some of the online programs I can only access with my work computer.

I take a moment to think about my colleagues in IT. I hope they have a big red telephone or something. An army of messenger pigeons, a horse or any other way of delivering notes between France and India, because that's where the majority of our IT team is now based.

I also take a moment to think about my IT Director, the one who sent all of those interminably long messages about the cyberattacks five weeks ago. 'We have resisted. Our security system is strong enough to resist to any cyber attack.' I don't need to remind you that pride is one of the seven sins.

I get a call and a message from my English colleague. I'll need to arrange another meeting with the job candidate. No problem, except I don't have their phone number or email address anymore. It was all on their resume, which of course was on my computer.

I can't believe I'm working by text message. The best thing at this point is surely just to leave the office and wait for the mess to be solved.

So I leave. I'm in the street. I'm walking towards the train station.

Time seems to be passing by really slowly. I feel like I'm finding time that I'd previously lost somehow. It's calm. Really calm.

There were no messages to read or to bother me (by choice) on my way home.

And suddenly, everything was quiet...

In 2008, Russia launched a military invasion on Georgia, before a wave of cyberattacks helped bring the already weakened country completely to its knees. The sheer size, coordination and sophistication of the attacks meant that it would have been impossible for an independent group of hackers to pull them off. It was almost certainly the work of a sovereign state, and all signs pointed to Russia.

South Korea was the next victim of large-scale cyberattacks in July 2009. Twenty-five websites, including the sites of the president, the minister of defense, the minister for foreign affairs, the Shinhan Bank and the Korea Exchange Bank were affected. Tensions with North Korea remained high throughout the attack. According to South Korean media, the National Intelligence Service believed that Pyongyang was indeed responsible, but they had no way of proving it.

ANOTHER COUP FOR PYONGYANG!

The next few days, in a large multinational corporation where all the channels of communication have been brutally severed...

The day after the attack.
Early morning: dazed and confused.

I thought as I woke up that it was all just a bad dream. It'll be over soon, if it weren't already. The show will be back on the road soon enough.

On my way to work I found myself staring blankly into my smartphone, that frankly isn't so smart anymore. More precisely I'm looking at my email inbox which has been frozen since 1.22 pm yesterday. The last two messages read: 'We have been the victim of a cyberattack. Shut down your computers.' And the one following that: 'Whatever you do, don't shut down your computer!'

Since then, nothing.

Just emptiness.

The darkness of the abyss.

Nothing to read. Nothing to get excited about. Nothing to work on. In one fell swoop, the entire contents of my online calendar had disappeared. I try to remember: what was on my agenda today? There's a black hole in my head, too. I vaguely remember I had two meetings, but no more than that.

I arrive. Silence reigns over the lobby area.

The receptionists look a little lost as they stare into the black screens of their PCs. The phones sit motionless on front of them, and on the other end of the receiver there is a hollow, empty silence. Nothing.

No dialing tone.

Nothing.

Is this for real? Seriously? A cyberattack did this? I thought an attack, you know, like... broke things. Windows, walls... something. Our computers are still intact (they look like they are anyway), the building is still standing, and us, the employees, we're still here and very much alive.

First of all, where are the pirates? There have been no reports of Johnny Depp embarking at the reception desk, as far as I know anyhow. No Schwarzenegger cyborg, either. This whole cyber-thing kind of makes me think about Terminator.

Especially the part where we see where the machines came from and that microchip which eventually brings about the destruction of all humanity. It makes me shiver. When my alarm went off as usual yesterday morning, I did not expect to be confronted with any of this mess. No way. It's probably better that I didn't, otherwise I'd never have gotten out of bed.

I mean, it's impossible. Not us. Not today, when I need to send my presentation to Karl-Hans in Germany for his meeting tomorrow in

Amsterdam. No. And to think that yesterday I'd even considered sending it to myself by email just in case , which I have done before. I specifically remember thinking, 'No. It'll be fine. What could possibly happen between now and tomorrow?' I'd even thought about sending it to Karl-Hans early that morning, but I kept getting distracted or had something more important to do first. I was joyously procrastinating. Now it's too late. Great.

Back to square one. In any case, even if I had sent the presentation to myself by email, I wouldn't have been able to access it anyway. And if Karl-Hans hasn't printed his e-ticket, it's going to be pretty tough for him to get the plane there.

Why us, though? Is someone mad at us for something? Do we have some sensitive files hidden somewhere? Is it a client that we annoyed somehow?

I take the elevator up to my office floor in a state of total confusion. I feel totally lost without these tools that had become such a ubiquitous element of my daily life. I'm disoriented, inexistent, unpowerful and empty. And the day has only just begun.

There's an eerie calm.

A few colleagues are wandering around the corridors. I'm doing the same. No one dares to speak to each other. We are acting as if nothing has happened. We don't want to acknowledge it.

The day after the attack.
Early afternoon: panic time.

The minutes tick by slowly and it's becoming a challenge to sit in silence, just waiting for something to happen.

The tension is rising. Panic is beginning to set in. Things need to start happening; we can't stay like this. I have to communicate. If I can't communicate, I am nothing. Or at least my work is nothing.

At lunchtime I decide to get hold of some of the phone numbers of my colleagues so we can discuss about what's going on. I'm not hungry anyway, plus if everything starts working again suddenly, I'd prefer to be in the starting blocks ready to get back to work. But before that, I need some numbers.

First problem: how am I going to get them when the company directory is online? The only way to access it is with my work computer (which is still very much on lockdown) or with my smartphone (which still has no access to our internal networks). I start thinking nostalgically about the big local phone directory we had at home when I was a child. I let myself drift into a daydream about all of these numbers listed one after the other, neatly organized in alphabetical order. No need to worry about viruses. The directory always worked perfectly. Except in the case of a fire. I remember the incredibly thin paper that you had to be so careful with when turning the page, otherwise you'd tear it. And there was the very particular scent of the ink on the paper that would float up off the oversized page and ignite my senses. You don't get

that when you search an online directory. I admit
that sometimes I'd stare for a little too long at
certain colleagues' profile photos. And I have
noticed that the photo of the girl on the 3rd floor
looks nothing like the real person I see in the
cafeteria during lunch.

I awaken from my daydream. Being in a
nostalgic trance like that at work is probably not a
good idea. Everything is still as silent as before.
There's nothing happening at all as the big black
empty screen of my computer constantly reminds
me.

Second problem: I've realized that I'm
going to need their cellphone numbers because
their company desk phones won't be working

either. It's been confirmed that this is now imperative as our fixed line phones are 'dead', 'done', 'screwed', and couple of other words that essentially mean they aren't going to be working any time soon. I know this to be the case because, when I look at the phones of the few people who actually still have one on their desk, I see that they're in basically the same state as our computers: off, kaput, silent, un-beeping. No power, no life, no nothing. Reduced to a mere plastic shell and a screen without light. Random colleagues from our floor pass from time to time to pick up the receiver and check if the dialing tone that will liberate us from our misery has come back. Nothing. The emptiness at the other end of line tells us that we have no link to the outside world, only to an eternal silence.

I remember the whole fuss when they switched our phones to having an IP. This meant that our voices would now be transmitted via the internet, and not using the old line we had before. I just hope that it still exists and we can somehow hook ourselves back up to it asap. But of course, our over-educated, over-qualified, super-talented, super-organized, and, above all, super-sure of themselves IT engineers never even thought for a quarter of a millisecond that the internet connection could one day be cut off, become blocked for some reason or another, or worse be attacked from the inside by some nefarious beast. And so here we are. Our line has been cut and nothing travels along it anymore. No data or files; no zeros or ones. Zilch. And now our voices can no longer be sent through the cable, even though it never asked to be transferred from its original line, where it was all safe and cozy and not bothering anyone.

I awaken from my daydream. It really isn't normal, to go off into a trance like that at work. The office is still silent. There is still less than nothing happening on the vast, dark ocean of a screen in front of me. It may be turned off, but for some reason I can't help but stare into its vast nothingness.

OK let's think about this. How can I get my hands on my colleagues' cellphone numbers?

We've received no news. That's probably got something to do with the fact that we have no way of receiving it. At least not through the usual channels of communication. You know, the ones we've gotten used to using every day of our lives for the past few years. Email, for example. I have a few chats with some of the people who work on my floor, and whom I barely know, and it seems that we're all in the exact same state of idleness. We've lost all direction and have no idea what to do, like little children awaiting instructions from their mistress. No one has seen the last remaining IT technician we have at the Strasbourg office. Our own boss is in New York this week. So, like most people on this dreary afternoon, I decide to go home and escape the anxiety of the whole situation. I'm sure everything will be back to normal tomorrow.

As I make my way home, my smartphone still turned off, only one thought is going through my head: this won't last too much longer. It can't. Something will be done about it soon. The IT guys have surely thought about this type of event occurring and they have back-up plan. Everything important has been saved somewhere, and in two shakes of a lamb's tail they'll get it all back up and running again. It's not that complicated, right? There must be an emergency server someplace, probably a lot of them in fact, where everything is isolated and protected from any type of intrusion at all. This time tomorrow we'll all have moved on and forgotten all about it. Definitely.

In the years 2009 and 2010, the western world was busy worrying about Iran's nuclear program. The media was constantly debating the likelihood of an Israeli intervention on at least one of the sites, all the while being careful to underline the considerable risks involved. Risks such as flying through the airspace of countries that would be against such an intervention, as well as the possibility of a disproportionate response from Iran, including the firing of long range missiles aimed at striking some of the largest cities in Israel.

A cyberattack that paralyzed the Bouchehr Nuclear Power Plant, on the other hand, would fulfil all of the same objectives without posing any risk to human life. Nor would it harm political relations or require military intervention. The only thing necessary would be a virus of sufficient sophistication to attack the central computer systems of the power station, the type of which both Israel and the United States were suspected to have already developed.

That virus was called Stuxnet. The Windows operating system recognized it as harmless. It utilized stolen digital security keys from technology companies in Taiwan. The malware was initially introduced to the system using an infected USB drive, therefore requiring a human accomplice. This was necessary as the internal computer system was not entirely connected to the 'outside world'. The malware took control of automated electromechanical processes, the electrical network and an entire complex control system created by German manufacturer Siemens. It went unnoticed for months, progressively causing more and more damage, including to the centrifuges which eventually were completely physically destroyed as a result of the attack. The development of a virus this sophisticated would have required an investment of many millions of dollars.

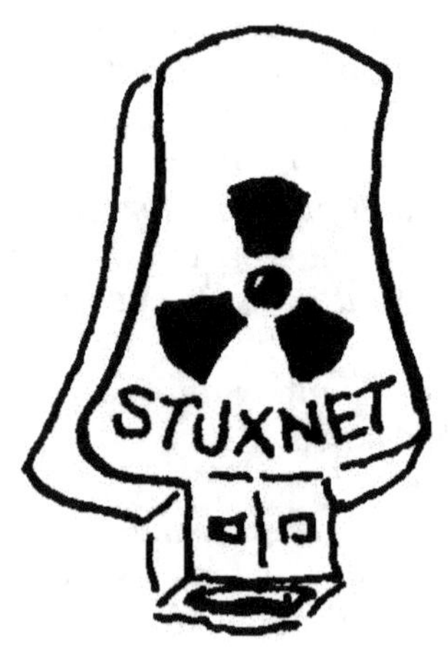

Two days since the attack.
Trauma time.

My alarm goes off. It's 6.30 am.

This morning feels different. That's because I'm now *post-trauma*. The emotions wash over me as soon as I wake. I feel like I've been brutally attacked. As if I have been the victim of an invasion. A personal one. It was just an invasion of a tool I use for work, but there is this feeling that I've somehow been personally violated. They invaded me too. I stay in my bed daydreaming for a few moments. There's no point in me hurrying to get up in any case. I can't use my computer and my calendar is totally empty. I can't even remember what I was supposed to be doing. It has been so long since I actually needed to use my memory, seeing as everything was automatically stored for me in my online agenda, that now it seems it just doesn't want to work anymore. Before, all I needed to do was open up my phone and I'd know where I was meant to be and how to get there, who I was meant to be with or talking to, what their contact details were and what time everything was supposed to be happening. No matter how much I fiddled with my not-so-smartphone though, the calendar remained empty. Nada. No meetings, no conference calls. Jack. My inbox: frozen. Still stuck on the message I received two days ago at 1. 22 pm: 'We have been the victim of a cyberattack. Shut down your computers.' And the one after: 'Whatever you do, don't shut down your computer!' These messages are just going around my head in a loop. Since then, we've heard nothing more. Literally nothing. A vast emptiness. Abyssal. Oceanic. Cosmic.

I get myself together again and gather my

thoughts. I decide that this would be a great day to take my time getting to work. I have a lovely slow breakfast, listen to the news and talk to my kids about what they'll be doing today. For once I'm not running around everywhere. And for once I'm not thinking about the tough meeting I've got later with the US. I amble gently to the train station. There are delays. I don't care. A packed train approaches. I take a few steps toward the back of the platform and decide I'll wait for the next. I don't even bother trying to get on. Usually it wouldn't matter to me. No matter how tight of a squeeze, somehow I'd get in that train; pushing people to the side just so I could get to the office five minutes earlier. Who cares if there are trains every five minutes anyway? The next one arrives. Also packed. No problem. I'll get the next one. It leaves.

I watch as the other passengers elbow their way onboard. They look like they'd kill their own mother and father just for a spot on that precious carriage! I actually feel a little sorry for them. The poor fools weren't lucky enough to be working for a company that was hit by a cyberattack two days ago. I'm the lucky one! At last it's me that gets to take my time. Doing what I want, at the pace I want.

Suddenly I get anxious. What sort of situation is awaiting me at the office? What will greet me as I pass through the lobby? Will I once again see a buzzing hive of activity? Or will I be dealt one more day of mind-crushing silence?

I enter the lobby.

It's silent. The receptionists are still looking

with empty eyes into their black monitors. I don't even dare to give them the cheerful 'hello!' that I usually do when I arrive in the mornings.

I stutter:

'Erm... He... hell... hello. Still nothing happening?'

'No. Still nothing.'

I sigh. Then I take a deep breath and smile.

'Ah well. I'm sure that today everything will get back online eventually. Have a great day!'

I step into the elevator and let it swallow me.

I arrive on my floor. There's a bunch of people gathered around the coffee machine. Unbelievable! It's stopped working, too! Five of us stare at it glumly without saying a word to one another, baffled and speechless. Even the coffee machine. What have we done to deserve this?

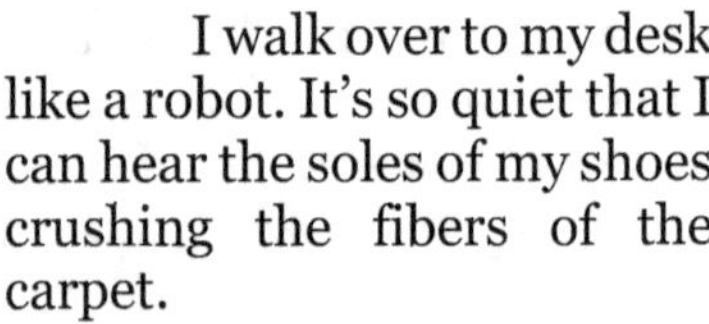

I walk over to my desk like a robot. It's so quiet that I can hear the soles of my shoes crushing the fibers of the carpet.

'Hi Christian.'

Christian's the guy who delivers the mail. Over the past few years he's seen the volume of his deliveries diminish considerably. He's worried he might even get fired and feels like he's on borrowed time. I mean, who uses paper anymore? Christian diligently pushed his cart containing two envelopes that needed a stamp and three other brown envelopes, the internal ones of the company. Due to the fact that the amount of 'real' mail needing to be delivered has been reduced to such a tiny trickle, Christian has had some new responsibilities bestowed upon him. Now it is also up to him to check that the coffee machines are working, put paper in the printers, order stationery and distribute entry passes to new arrivals. His job has changed a lot. And in spite of everything, he still arrives, and leaves, with a big smile on his face.

Silence. Total silence. Utter silence.

The enormous multifunctional machine that is the office's photocopier/printer/scanner no longer makes a sound. This thing that usually sits there purring gently. Quietly she hums, even through the night as she waits for us all to arrive the next morning when she begins swallowing sheets of paper and shooting them out into the tray on her side. She's resting this morning, though. Taking a break. Hibernating, like a giant tortoise.

Even after giving my smartphone a good shake, it still refuses to make a sound. Not even a little beep to let me know I've received a message. No reassuring vibrations to tell me I've got a meeting in a few minutes. No ringtone to let me know I've got an incoming call, routed through my computer (still hopelessly turned off), that would make me look super important as I take the call using my headset and microphone. No more wasted seconds performing that oh-so outdated gesture of actually picking up the handset. The ring-ring of the old gray telephones resonates nowhere but in the heads of those who have nothing better to do than think about how 'things were better before all this digital nonsense'. Like the click you'd hear when you put the handset down onto the little plungers that would cut the dialing tone, or make it sound as you lifted the receiver off. The gatekeeper of the line.

A deafening silence.

I think about the years during our long transition from paper to digital. The library gradually became a wasteland. Some wiseass has now stuck a note on the wall outside: 'This library still exists! There are real books, newspapers and journals that you can actually touch. If you want to, you're free to take a look at them.' There was an air of revenge about it. Under other circumstances, I admit it may have been kinda funny. But right now, it's only reminding me of the fact that somehow we've lost everything. That we've thrown it all away.

I walk down another corridor. People have left their office doors open. I glance at the screen of a colleague. And there, upon the black monitor, in a big red pop-up window:

'Ooops, your files have been encrypted! Your important files are encrypted. Many of your documents, photos, videos, databases and other files are no longer accessible because they have been encrypted. Maybe you are busy looking for a way to recover your files, but do not waste your time. Nobody can recover your files without our decryption service.'

Woah! They're talking to us. We've really been attacked. So what do we say to this pirate, this ransom merchant? This bandit who has stolen our data and put it into a digital blender, hit the power button and mixed it up until it's just an indecipherable soup of nonsense. This crook who now wants us to pay them an unbelievable amount of money just so they can unscramble the eggs for us, so to speak.

I won't be trying to recuperate any of the data from this computer, which belongs to Jean-Louis, as I have very little interest in it personally. I'll leave that to him. Yep, Jean-Louis' data is worth about the same amount *souped* or *unsouped*, such is this man's prodigious lack of productivity. When you mix the wind with the air - which is precisely what Jean-Louis did all day, producing 'slides' that would have contained a considerable amount more zeros than ones - you don't come up with anything more interesting than an empty draft, dear pirate. So he can keep that big empty space, that vast expanse of nothingness, that black hole which occupies the gigabytes of Jean-Louis' computer. After all, if you multiply zero by zero, you'll end up with nothing, no matter how many times you do it - or how much it costs. At least this little court jester is having fun, prancing down the corridor giggling as he juggles with his zeros.

Anyway, where was I? It seems like today is going to be just as long and just as painful as yesterday. I start getting used to the idea that 'this nuisance' isn't going to go away soon. Our scallywag, it appears, might actually know what he's doing.

I'm just going to tidy the papers on my desk one more time and then we'll see what happens tomorrow.

CHEERS FOR YER TREASURE!
SCREW YOU!

Three days since the attack.
Back online, but still no Internet...

I arrive at my desk. My computer is still desperately lifeless. I see a little piece of paper looking a little out of place. There's writing scrawled upon it. It's a list of names. Then I remember: I spent three hours yesterday looking for the numbers of my colleagues and other people that I need to talk to. Time has become only an abstract concept. At some point, within what I would call 'a reasonable amount of time', I'm going to need to talk to these people, whether it be in a few minutes or a few hours, or even days. I need to get on with my work! I've got things to do and other things I need taken care of. That being said, my idea of what constitutes 'getting things done' has changed considerably. I'm a lot less ambitious now; my standards have been lowered. A lot. What's the point in any case? Nothing else is happening.

I take a look at my piece of paper. There are five names and five numbers. I need to find about fifty more. I start feeling a little demoralized. It took me three hours to find five numbers, so finding fifty is going to be hard. These are cellphone numbers we're talking about. Landline numbers are useless now. I calculate that it would take me a little over a century to redo the whole company directory. To hell with productivity - I need to prioritize!

I need to think clearly. I'm in a situation I never expected to be in. I have no idea how to get out of it and none of the tools I would usually have to do it. I'm pretty sure, too, that no one else had envisaged a situation like this happening. Even Dominic. Or I should say, especially Dominic. What exactly is/was his job anyway? OK, so he sent out a few messages, but they left me under the impression that is weren't so much a case of 'if', but rather 'when'. And I'm pretty sure he'd never planned for anything like this happening, where everything stopped working all at once and there being no way at all for anyone to communicate with one another. Because if he had thought of it, this whole mess would have been solved way before the three days that have passed already. We would've at least switched to some sort of back-up system. Whatever he had envisaged, it wasn't even nearly as catastrophic or apocalyptic as this.

I begin to wonder what the directors are doing. How they are planning to move forward, starting with the IT team. Dominic is based in Amsterdam and our CEO is in Madrid. Except for small local teams, the large majority of our IT force is based in either Portugal or India. I wonder how they're managing to talk to one another. Surely they've all met up someplace to discuss this shambles. Because right now, it must all seem like a giant mess to them. I still don't really understand exactly what happened, but after watching some TV last night, I've basically managed to comprehend that this little beast isn't exactly friendly and that it has absolutely destroyed the IT networks of many large companies. For some reason, in this type of situation, I always think of an Englishman sat on top of a pile of rubble, smoking a cigar and calmly drinking a cup of tea. The famous British stiff upper lip. Well, there are a few Brits on the board of directors. They should help us get through the chaos.

I've made no advances with my hunt for numbers. I've just remembered that in ten days we're supposed to have a meeting in Brussels to revise our commercial strategy for one of our product lines. Something like fifty people are supposed to take part in  the meeting, coming from all over the world. If someone doesn't get our computers back up and running again soon, there's going to be a whole lot of catching up to do to make up for what we've missed in the last few days. Or maybe there'll be nothing at all to do, in fact. I really need to get in touch with my boss in Geneva to decide if we're actually going to go ahead with the meeting or not, given the circumstances. Back to work, then. I need to find my boss' number then the list of attendees. Which I don't have. I don't remember the last time I actually printed something, and it was Brussels that handled the meeting invitations. So first of all I need to get hold of the number for the Belgian team.

Time to fire up the neurons. How can I find these numbers?
Wait, I just got a text.

'Hi Angeline. It's Patrick. I just got hold of your number. So here's mine. Patrick Duchemin.'

I immediately call Patrick, who's based in Lyon.

Patrick picks up after less than half a ring.
'Patrick, I'm so happy you answered! It's

Angeline. How's it going for you all in Lyon?'

'Well, we're not exactly partying. It's not like anyone's totally in panic, but we're a little worried. We have no clue what's happening. No word from anyone. We got no way to even talk to people. What about Strasbourg?'

'Not great here either. We don't know what to do, really. We're just waiting. We're pretty optimistic that it'll be over soon, though. All these black screens arc pretty depressing to be honest. You have any news?'

'Nothing. They asked us to shut down the computers on Tuesday, just like you. Since then we've heard nothing. Victor, our boss, hasn't been too chatty. I think he's worried. From what I've heard, all the bosses are going to have a call tonight to talk about it. All we really know is just don't do anything. Call clients so they know we haven't gone AWOL. I think everything will be back up and running by the weekend.'

'OK, well, I guess we'll see. Martine isn't here at the moment. You know she was named office manager at the beginning of the month? She's been in the US this week. She'll be back tomorrow, I think. She should be able to tell us more. It's going to be a real baptism of fire for her if it carries on any longer like this! She's going to regret taking the job! By the way, how do you get my number? I'd like to know because I need to contact a bunch of people, starting with John in Geneva, to see what's going on with the Brussels meeting in ten days. I don't really know where I should start looking. Do you think we've got a paper version of the phone directory?'

'I have the exact same problem and the same questions! I got your number from your email signature. It was lucky that you sent me a mail just before all this happened. It was one of the few that I could still see. You might be able to find John's on the company website. I think all of the directors have to have their number there in case clients need to contact them.'

'OK. I'm gonna check that. That's if the website is still working!'

'It is. Weirdly, but thankfully, it's still up. A client told me this morning.'

'OK great. Thanks, Patrick. It's reassuring to talk to someone. I've been feeling a bit lonely! I have a lot of colleagues around me here, but the truth is I work more with you and people on the other side of the world than I do with people on my floor! Anyway, I'll leave you to it. I really need to get hold of John. And the other people coming to Brussels. It's going to take me hours. Even if I do find them then I'll have to call them all too.'

'OK good luck. If you want you can send me a few of the names that you need to find. Maybe I can find a couple of them here, in my address book or something. At least it'll give me something to do!' Patrick added, laughing.

'Perfect, thank you. Have a good day. Say hi to Lyon.'

'Thanks. You too. Bye.'

How have the directors managed to organize a conference call? I'll figure that out later. First I need to go on the company website from my phone. I don't need to explain to you that a cellphone's screen is pretty small and not very practical for working on. But I'm not going to complain - at least it works. After a few minutes' hunting, I eventually find the page with the details of all the main product managers, listed in alphabetical order. I scroll down and find John's profile. A wave of relief. His cellphone number is there. I write it down immediately on my scrap of paper and enter it into my phone. I write him a text.

'Hello John. It's Angeline. Would you have a minute so we can talk? I'd like to discuss what we're going to do for the meeting in Brussels that's supposed to happen in ten days. Are we going ahead with it? If you'd like to cancel, we'll need to tell everyone by Monday.'

That's one of the longest texts I've ever written. I don't know why, but there's a little voice at the back of my head telling me that this is only the beginning. Things are going to get a lot harder from now on.

While I wait for John to reply, I'll try and locate the numbers for my other colleagues in Brussels. OK... let's see... Cate, of course. But what's her last name again? And is it Cate or Kate? Damn it, I don't remember.

I text Patrick. 'Patrick. You wouldn't have Cate's number, would you? I can't remember her last name. She's the communications manager in Brussels.'
I wait for his reply.

Patrick: 'Kate Vandevelde? I don't have it. Going to look.'

Ah that's it! Kate Vandevelde. And luckily for me, I'm able to find the number for Jane Smith, who works on the same team as her, on my phone.

She's the communications manager in London.

I text Jane: 'Hi Jane. It's Angeline from Strasbourg. I'm desperately trying to get in touch with Kate Vandevelde in Brussels. You don't have her number by any chance?'

I wait for her reply.

This is taking a long time. It's already 11 am and I'm moving as fast as a snail going through glue. Still nothing from John. But what am I doing? Why don't I just call him? I usually talk to him by email or chat. He's so busy though, it's almost impossible to have a call with him unless you've booked it beforehand and there's something very specific you need to talk to him about. Given the current circumstances though, there's a chance he'll answer. She who dares wins. It's worth a try.

Connecting... dialing...
Ring one ...
Ring two...

'Hello. John speaking.'
'Oh, hello John! Thanks for answering. It's Angeline here. How are you? Did you see my text about the meeting in Brussels? What do you think?'
'Oh, hi Angeline. I'm about to have a call with the crisis team. I can't talk right now. Could

you call me at 1.30?'

> 'Sure. I'll call you at 1.30. Talk to you later.'
> 'Thanks Angeline. Goodbye.'

Well, there you go. I managed to talk to John directly using a telephone. And I have an appointment for call with him at 1.30 pm. That's my entire day. It makes a change from having one call after another without even a couple of minutes to go to the restroom.

Where should I note our meeting, now that I don't have an agenda? The one on my smartphone is empty and I'm not sure if I'm allowed to use it. I write it down on a Post-it. If this goes on for much longer, I'll go out and buy a real agenda from the office supplies store around the corner. I stick the Post-it onto my computer screen. I can use it as a message board now. At least it can be good for something.

11.30 am already! I've done nothing. Literally nothing. And it's 11.30 am. I really need to making progress with this list. Whatever happens, I'm sure John's going to need it to make his decision. I can remember a few names by memory, but there's no way I'll be able to figure out all of them like that. I need to talk to Kate. No news from Jane or Patrick.

I receive a text: 'Hi Angeline. It's Vincent in Lille. I just got hold of your number. You don't happen to have Patrick's in Lyon do you? I really need to speak to him for a client meeting tomorrow.'

I quickly add Vincent Brulé to my contacts. Now I have four names, with Jane, Patrick and John. Slowly but surely I'm getting there.

Text to Vincent: 'Hi Vincent. Thanks for getting in touch. Here's Patrick's number. Do you have Kate Vandevelde's number in Brussels by any chance?'

Vincent: 'Kate Vandevelde +32 987589591.'

Perfect! I call Kate.

'Kate Vandevelde.'

'Kate, hello, this is Angeline in Strasbourg. How's everything going in Brussels?'

'Hi Angeline. Well, a bit weird really. We still don't have a clue what's happening. And to be honest, the longer the goes on, the less convinced I am they're going to be able to fix it. We're OK for now, but if it's still like this on Monday, it's going to start getting really serious.'

'I hear you. Kate, I'm calling you because I'll be speaking with John at 1.30 pm about the meeting in ten days. We need to decide if we're going to go ahead with it or not. I really need to get my hands on the list of people who are supposed to be coming, but obviously I've got no access to anything. A perfect situation, huh?! Anyway, it's me who's supposed to be organizing everything, but I thought that because it was you who took care of the reservations that you might have it?

'I'll check with Melissa. Actually she was the one looking after that. She's in the next office. I'll ask her and then I'll let you know.'

12.15 pm. At this rate, it's going to take me an eternity. And for now I can't do much more. I'm going to use this time to take a walk and get some lunch. At least it'll give me something to do. It should help me relax a little, and maybe give me the chance to get to know my office neighbor Paul. I know he's lost for things to do, too.

1.30 pm. I come back to the office to call John. I had a nice lunch. And I'm really glad I took the time to talk to Paul, who takes care of the Strasbourg office's finances. I learned about all of the exciting things happening in his department, and he also answered my questions about how they come up with the budgets. I left with the impression that we both felt a little less lonely after the utter chaos we've been facing over these past few days. Apparently though, the people in finance are really starting to panic, because if the system isn't back online by Monday, they won't be able to invoice our clients at the end of the month.

Text from John:
'Angeline, I'm sorry. I can't talk now. Call me at around 3 pm instead.'

'OK, no problem.'

I don't even need to check my agenda because I don't have one. I know without a shadow of a doubt that I have nothing at three, seeing as there is nothing to do and I haven't done anything in three days now.

1.45 pm. Text from Kate with photo attached. An MMS. 'Hi Angeline. You're in luck. Melissa had printed the list of participants for your meeting. I took a photo of it for you. Hope it helps.'

Amazing! A blurry photo sent by text of a list of meeting attendees. In 2017. Unbelievable. But, to be honest, at this point nothing surprises me.

I zoom in on the tiny photo. Damn. Only names and email addresses. Not one phone number.

I carefully copy the list of names onto a sheet of A4 paper. I realize that my handwriting looks terrible. It's been so long since I last wrote more than a couple of lines on a piece of paper using a pen that I've forgotten how to do it.

2.45 pm. List finished. Now I just need to find their numbers. I head straight to the website again to get the names of the three directors, whom I deduce must be on there just like John. I find Brian Callum and Vincent Martin without any problems. But for some unknown reason, Alexander Tyndon's number is nowhere to be seen.

3 pm. I call John, who picks up after one ring. There must be something terribly wrong if he

answers that quickly.

'Angeline, I guess you're calling me about the meeting in Brussels? Let's do it quickly because I'm jumping on a plane to meet the crisis team. Have you been able to get in contact with the participants? What are we doing?'

Would you listen to him! I don't think he has any idea how this has affected my productivity.

'John, listen. It's not that easy. I've managed to get hold of a list of the participants from Kate in Brussels but now I need to find some way of contacting them all. In my opinion, I'm not sure, but I think if we don't manage to sort everything out very quickly then everyone is going to be busy doing something else anyway over the next few weeks.'

'Will we get cancelation fees?'

'At this point I don't have a clue, frankly. I'd need access to the reservation confirmations. But I'm thinking that the longer this all takes, the less likely that's going to be.'

'OK, Angeline. Listen, let's cancel it, like you suggest. It's better that way. We'll reschedule for the end of July or beginning of September. The priority right now is for you to call everyone and let them know so they can cancel their trips. I've got to go. Let me know how you're getting along.'

'OK.'

'Oh, and try to create a WhatsApp group so everyone is in the loop. We've just done the same for the directors. It's a good way for us all to communicate while the systems are down.'

'Good idea. But I thought we'd been told not to use WhatsApp for security reasons?'

'Yes that's true, Angeline, you're right. But given the current situation, I think we don't have much choice. I think some of the directors used it for the first time yesterday, to be honest. They'd never heard of it before we created our group! But keep that to yourself OK?'

'Sure, don't worry. But honestly, that doesn't really surprise me. Anyway, I'll leave you to it I know you must be busy. And I'd better go, I've got a lot to do, too!'

'OK, let's keep in touch. Good luck. Bye.'

'See you. Good luck to you too.'

As soon as we hang up, I realize that the call felt like I was taking to just another colleague, not a director. Is this debacle actually bringing us all closer together? Surely it is better to stay together through these tough times, as equals. Cohesive. The fact he suggested a WhatsApp group is pretty funny. Not to mention a very good idea. It doesn't change the fact that I need to find fifty numbers for the people coming to Brussels, however, or try and find them on WhatsApp even if they already do have an account. Well, almost fifty names.

It's 3.15 pm, and I've done almost nothing. At least that's the impression I have, considering what time it is. And yet somehow I'm exhausted.

Wait, what's happening? I've just received five text messages and two WhatsApp invitations.

'Hello, it's Carl Bellamy from the London office. I'm writing this message to all of my contacts to try and get hold of the number for Valentine Vermeil in Strasbourg'.

'Hello, it's Andrew Smith in Brighton. Does anyone have the number for Cornelius Kehling in Munich? It's urgent. It's for a pitch we're presenting to a client tomorrow.'

'Anyone have the number for Marco Menoni in the Milan office? It's urgent. Chris Brown (New York)'.

'Message from Valentine Vermeil to all of her contacts: does anyone have Andrew Smith's number?'

'Hi. It's Cornelius Kehling, from the Munich office. I need to get hold of Peter Van der Trak in Amsterdam to finalize a pitch. Does anyone have his cellphone number? Also, I've created a WhatsApp group for everyone working on the Werter project. If you know anyone who's involved, it would be great if you could forward them this message.'

What's all this? I don't mind helping out a few colleagues, but I've got my own numbers to find! OK, I'll be nice. I send Cornelius Kehling's number to Andrew Smith. I then add the numbers of the people I've received texts from to my contact list. You never know. As I leave that evening, I'll try and remember to tell Valentine Vermeil that Carl Bellamy was trying to get hold of her. I'll give her his number in case she doesn't have it. Phone number exchanger. It appears I have a new job.

4 pm. In a text message, I write the names of the 42 people coming to Brussels for whom I still don't have a number. That's fifty, minus John, Vincent and Brian, plus five others whose numbers I fortunately had in my address book already. I send the text out to all of my colleagues asking if they too could help me out with any of the numbers on my list. It's a bit message-in-a-bottle, but I don't really have much choice.

5.30 pm. I'm exhausted. It's quite the experience, working by text message. Not exactly productive. Anyway, it's time to go home. Today has already been too much, emotionally speaking.

6 pm. I'm on the train. Damn! I forgot to go and see Valentine Vermeil.

*But where on Earth could this beast have come
from?*

According to the American company Akamai Technologies, in the second quarter of 2014, the top ten countries identified as the source of cybercrime are:

1 China: 43% of attacks
2 Indonesia: 15%
3 USA: 13%
4 Taiwan : 3.7%
5 India: 2.1%
6 Russia: 2%
7 Brazil: 1.7%
8 South Korea: 1.4%
9 Turkey: 1.2%
10 Romania: 1.2%

I vaguely remember having a meeting during which our manager mentioned a few of the countries on this list, stating that they were aware of their hacking activities, that they were unsure what to do about it and that if we had any ideas, they would be most welcome. For the moment though, we'd be treating this as a low priority as there was no real immediate threat. We'll discuss it more at a later date.

Well, we all know what happened next, don't we? We've seen it happen live, in real time.

The worm got inside. The appropriately-named malware broke through our defenses. It snuck in through a door left slightly ajar, or one of the many windows in our internal network's wall; the wall that was supposed to protect us from the outside world.

In order to get in, it had to be very small, very thin, and, above all, very discreet. Perhaps it lay dormant in some nook or cranny for a while, biding its time, waiting for the right moment to attack. It sniffed around and found that it smelled good. There was a delicious pile of fresh data that it would relish the opportunity to feed upon.

Slowly, the worm slithered its way through the pipes that connect us all. As it made its pernicious journey, it devoured any data it came across. First it would capture it, then toss it around to make sure it was all nice and mixed up, then it would bundle it up and lock it away tightly in a safe. Each safe had its own code that only the worm knew. If it didn't know what the data was or how to lock it up, it would simply destroy it.

To think that it got into my computer. My unprotected computer.

I imagine this little thing slithering around as fast as it can, scurrying into all of the darkest corners of our servers, destroying everything in its path and gobbling up as much data as its greedy self could manage. It must have been drooling with pleasure as it made its way around our network, full of big, fat, juicy data. Unique or duplicated, confidential or public. It gorged itself until it became obese, stuffed full like a force-fed goose. It became so fat that there was no way it would be able to leave through the same tiny door it came in.

I feel horrible even thinking about it. There I was, working happily and minding my own business, as this enormous beast was doing its dirty work just in front of me, eagerly swallowing my precious work. My precious Excel and PowerPoint presentations were all part of its enormous buffet.

Then, suddenly, the lights went out. The shutters were pulled down to prevent this thing from spreading. The beast was trapped.

But what do we send down the pipes to kill it?

In 2011, a second more complex worm appeared. Known as Flame, it seemed to have some relation to Stuxnet.

In May of that year, it was Lockheed Martin's turn, the enormous US defense contractor and notably the manufacturer of the F-22 Raptor jet fighter. They were the victim of a serious cyberattack, the origin of which remains unknown. Its entire information network was paralyzed for hours after attackers exploited Lockheed's VPN login system. The hackers had managed to acquire the codes of the company's SecurID hardware fobs that were used by employees to log in to their network remotely.

In June 2011, it was revealed that many hundreds of Gmail accounts of high-ranking US government workers, Chinese dissidents, Asian diplomats, soldiers and journalists had been hacked. According to Google, the location of the origin of the attack was Jinan, home to a Chinese military base, as well as a school founded with the support of the Chinese military. The school had already been accused by Google of attempted hacking activity. China denied the accusations.

In September 2011, a wave of attacks targeting government websites was orchestrated in Japan.

In June 2012, up to $80 million was stolen in a wave of cyberattacks that hit US, European and Latin American banks.

Four days after the attack.
Holding on.

A note was posted next to the coffee machine during the night.

On happiness, by Alain

A therapy

'Me, said the other, for fifteen days I've been doing some happiness therapy, and I feel very good. There are times when my thoughts become acrid, when I criticize everything furiously and I see nothing with any beauty or good; in others or in myself. When you tend towards this way of thinking, it means you need to do some happiness therapy. It consists of using your good mood against all types of misfortune, and especially against small things that might otherwise leave you cursing, if indeed you weren't doing happiness therapy. Well, on the contrary, these little worries can be useful, like a hill helps you to build your thigh muscles.

'There are,' the other continued, 'boring people who gather together to complain and whine. Normally we would flee from them, but with happiness therapy, on the contrary, we seek them out; they are like springs for doing gymnastics at home. After pulling the smaller ones to begin, we are able to stretch the bigger ones.

'These things,' the other continued again, 'can also be good too, but just bad enough to be happiness therapy. A burned ragout, some old bread, the sun, some dust, accounts that need doing, an almost-empty purse; these are precious exercises. In boxing or fencing, for example, we say: 'I'm about to take a huge hit; either I parry it or I take it cleanly.' Normally, we would start wailing, like children, and we're so ashamed of wailing that we wail even more. But with happiness therapy, things happen completely differently; we receive the thing like a nice shower, we shake ourselves, we raise the shoulders in two steps, we stretch the muscles, they become softer, we throw one on top of the other like wet clothes; and so the stream of life flows as if from a liberated source, there is an appetite, the laundry is done, life feels good. But here, I say, I will leave you. Now you are blossoming; you're no longer any good for my happiness therapy.'

Good luck everyone. Signed someone from our floor.

I feel better now after this lovely bit of reading and source of serenity. It was a little long, but no matter, I now finally have time to read long pieces of writing. Anyway, back to work, in a good mood!

I need to be in a good mood, too, because I have a whole bunch of text messages to read. All on the tiny screen of my phone. Not to mention the numerous WhatsApp notifications I now have, as it happens most of which are to join one of the many other chat groups that have now formed.

I'll take a look at all that later. Right now my priority is to contact the people invited to the Brussels meeting. That means I need to carefully go through all of the messages I received in response to my own text last night.

I discover that out of the remaining 46 number I need, I've received 24. That's not too bad. Now there are only 22 numbers which I quickly realize will be a lot harder to find than I had first imagined.

The first problem I discover is that not all of the participants are fortunate to have a company smartphone (or the number that goes with it). I begin to daydream again and start wondering if having a cellphone makes us one of the lucky ones, or the contrary? When I think of all the misery it has brought me, I realize that perhaps it's not such a good thing at all. A few of my preexisting contacts have sent me the personal numbers of colleagues on my list. I've no idea how or why they would have these in the first place. I do find it a bit uncomfortable contacting colleagues on their personal phones, but I don't really have a choice.

I also create my very own WhatsApp using all of the numbers I have on my piece of paper, which is steadily and reassuringly getting darker as time passes and names are added. It gives me a feeling that I haven't experienced in a while; that something is really getting done. I can see the results of what I'm doing. I call my group 'Brussels Meeting Group'. Not very creative, but it gets the job done. Some of the colleagues for whom I've used a personal number appear with photos that are clearly intended for friends rather than colleagues; in their bathing suit, holding a fishing rod or a nice family photo posing with their kids.

Adding all of the names is a lot of work. But considering the amount of time that's already been wasted, and the fact that doesn't seem any closer to being resolved, there's no other choice but to tackle the task at hand with the tools that are available.

It's already midday. I've made progress, but I'm not out of the woods yet. This is confirmed when I discover that three of the meeting's participants were supposed to be coming from Australia. With the time difference and the time it takes for them to travel here, I really need to contact them as soon as possible.

I once again feel exhausted, even though it's only lunch time and I've done almost nothing. I think about the long career I've had, the high-level education and all of my experience and responsibilities, all so I could sit here writing out a list of names. It's pretty depressing. I decide that I'll have lunch out of the office today. It'll help to clear my head. Obviously for the past week my lunch breaks have been a little longer than usual.

I come back to the office and I'm feeling good. I feel like I can breathe again. My stomach isn't making any gargling or rumbling sounds. I have no indigestion from eating too quickly in front of my computer screen.

It's time to work.

Questions are beginning to appear from a few people in the WhatsApp group, which now has 30 people in it. Not bad. Usually everyone seems too busy to respond to my questions. Not anymore.

I send them a message:

'Hello everyone. John and I are trying to decide what to do about the upcoming meeting in Belgium. It's highly probable that we'll have to cancel, given what's going on. I'll let you know. I need the numbers for David Morton (Dubai), Stacia Willem (Luxemburg), Vladimir Aztinovitch (Moscow) and Carola Liu (Beijing). If any of you have any of these numbers, please send them over! Angeline.'

Text to John:

'Hi, John. Just to let you know that I've created the WhatsApp group as you can see with almost everyone from the Brussels meeting in it. There are a few more people to add but it should be done by this evening. So what are we going to do about the meeting?'

Reply from John five minutes later:

'Angeline, I think we should cancel. The problem is more serious than we had first thought. We need to be working with our clients. I'll let you take care of it.'

'OK.'

OK John. 'I'll let you take care of it'? I don't think John quite realizes the conditions we've been working under for the past few days. I had been to talk to my colleagues in accounting a little while before John's message. They can't do anything, even though they've finally tidied their office, something they've been putting off for literally years now. They're currently outside working on the patio, with one of them showing the others some of the more advanced features of Excel. They're doing this on their personal computers. A few people have started bringing their own laptops so they can at least get some work done. All the while I've been straining my eyes using my smartphone for the past few days. I know that there are millennials who have managed to create billion dollar businesses with only the phone they have in their pocket, but I'm not a millennial and this is all making me sweat, rather than making me money. I'm from a generation of big screens, oral communication and visual contact. I've already made a huge effort these past few years, going from having meetings with people in the same room to virtual meetings where the participants are each on different sides of the planet. But this is asking too much. My ability to adapt has its limits. This is just way, way too far!

Back to the work at hand. How am I going to sort this out? I'm not used to working by text and WhatsApp. I still really need to get hold of Stacia Willem in Luxemburg. No one has her number. She was only hired recently, as far as I remember. That might explain why no one has her contact details. Oh wait! We connected on LinkedIn a few weeks ago. I can send her a message there.

What am I doing, contacting my own colleagues on LinkedIn? Seriously.

I think the best thing to do is to call each person individually. It'll take a long time, sure, but then at least I'll know that everyone has gotten the message that the meeting's been canceled. I'll post in on the WhatsApp group too, of course.

I spend the rest of the afternoon calling the participants. Almost all of them answered immediately. I used the opportunity to talk to everyone about the general situation in their office. Like us, they were struggling but managing to keep things afloat. I left a few messages; mostly for the people who would have been sleeping due to the time zone difference.

It's Friday afternoon, four days after the attack, and everyone's getting ready to leave for the weekend. A message arrives via WhatsApp, now our sole method of communication. I receive the same message multiple times due to the number of groups I'm in. It demonstrates the lack of organization we're facing, the fact that no one has taken hold of the situation and created one centralized, consolidated message group for this situation.

The message is from the crisis team, who have decided to name themselves the 'Gold Team'. They'd better live up to it. Let's see what they had to say to us:

****

For your information - confidential – do not share:

Here's a short summary of the position. We realise that progress might seem slow, but we can assure you that we are indeed making good progress and remain on course for getting our email up and running by the beginning of next week. We are grateful for your patience and that of your teams – so please do pass this message on as soon as you can so our people do not feel in the dark.

We're dealing with a new form of sophisticated and pernicious virus which we believe emanates from an attack on the Ukraine and was introduced via an online payroll system.

So far as we can tell, there has been no violation of confidential data and our systems have protected us well in that respect. We have included a statement to that effect on the website. Recipients of our emails and documents will have no cause for concern once the system is back up and running.

A large proportion of our computers that were infected by the virus will need to be completely reconfigured in order to be ready to be used.

We have made sufficient progress in order to be able to confirm email service on mobiles should be restored by the beginning of next week. This will include access to full data and the only action required by users will be a password change.

We will also have emergency access to data

on the internal network.

Also at the beginning of next week, we will relaunch the network, on an office by office basis, reinstate wireless and the ability for unaffected computers to log on to the network, though there will be limits to usage for capacity reasons.

We are working on a clear guidance note which explains all of the above and we will share this with you later.

A communications plan is being developed in conjunction with external PR/crisis management advisers.

The Gold Team
****

I forward this message to my other groups on WhatsApp just like everyone else has done, meaning everyone is now receiving the same message multiple times in different groups from different people. I think people are just doing it because they have nothing else to keep them occupied.

This update didn't really tell us much. It's kind of like telling us that the sun will rise tomorrow and that after the rain comes nicer weather. But, on the bright side, it seems that we will have a lot of things working again at the beginning of next week. I like the way they described people as being 'in the dark'. As if these attackers somehow turned out the lights. It's also clear from the very fact that this was told to us by WhatsApp that we're going to need some new channels that will enable us to communicate more efficiently!

We all just hope that this precious metal team has what it takes to manage this crisis, and that above all, they have the know-how that will allow us to start working again as soon as possible. Our clients won't wait too long before going to look for help with one of our competitors.

It's the weekend, and here I am thinking about all that's been going on during the past week. It's funny to think that last weekend I was going about my business as usual, and all the while these conspirators were plotting their crime. Now that the dust has settled, I'm sitting here wondering if I'll even have a job to go back to Monday.

The Gold Team obviously sent their message out believing that it would reassure us. Everything should soon be getting back to normality. They want us to know that our IT teams are doing all they can to make sure this happens over the weekend, but I'm not so sure though that things are as 'fine' as they're telling us. If they were, our IT team must be working extremely hard; like never before, one could say.

WhatsApp groups are blossoming like daisies in a meadow on the first day of spring this Monday morning. A new one sprouts up for every hour that passes by. It's actually quite welcome after this rather anxiety-ridden weekend.

- Human Resources friends group
- Finance community
- Whose-it project
- Team Milan
- 6th floor Amsterdam
- Attack news
- Emergency IT
- Suggestions for banking clients
- Client reception 3rd floor Frankfurt
- How to deal with invoices @ end of month
- Client suggestions
- How to get an e-ticket without email
- Talk to Paris reception
- Urgent numbers
- Tips and tricks to help you out - IT Madrid

I don't know which way to look. I'm getting messages and invitations from groups that I have absolutely no business being in. And of course, each time any one of them writes the smallest of messages, I get a notification. Still, I guess it beats silence.

What this dramatic (as some would call it) situation is demonstrating, is that whatever happens in life, whether personal or professional, things will always work out. We just need to keep going. Right now, there is a business to get back up and running, and good golly we're going to do it.

It's Monday morning, and after a briefing at reception by the office manager Martine (who is finally back from the States), I've rediscovered a certain sense of how people continually and collectively reinvent the ways to make things work when faced with a crisis. This feeling comes to me not so much in a nostalgic but rather in a childlike manner.

The directors have asked us to join them for a drink to celebrate the summer vacation period which is coming up[2]. The internal communications department had no other choice but to go to each and every floor sticking hand written notes up on the walls:

'Don't forget to come for drinks on July 7, starting at 6 pm'. Each note was surrounded by hand drawn and colored flowers. It was like being at school again, but wow, so much better than a dry, boring, black and white impersonal email!

Having spent years in almost-silent protest fighting for their right to exist in the face of online

---

[2] In France, a large proportion of the country takes a vacation in August.

sources, our friends in the office library have once again found a raison d'être. It could be seen as a little 'passive-aggressive' on their part to have posted on each floor a handwritten list of all the works and articles currently available, with each title carefully highlighted.

The weirdest thing keeps happening, too. When I call my colleagues on the telephone, they actually pick up! It's been years since that happened. The best you can hope for these days when you call someone is to reach their voicemail. Everyone is so busy that they need to have multiple phones, (personal, professional, mobile and landline), at least two email addresses and various other messaging tools. Yet paradoxically you can never get hold of anyone. If there were ever any proof that these electronic devices that were supposed to bring us all closer to one another were actually pushing us toward an ever more isolated existence, this is it. Lose all the email addresses and let everyone only have one number and people would suddenly be more available to talk.

It's getting noisy in the corridors again. People are talking to each other. I swear I've even heard laughter. We are human again. At least, I think we are.

There's some kind of training course happening, so I go down to take a look. Normally there's absolutely no way I would have gone. No time, too many things to do. But to my surprise, every single invitee is there, without exception. The typical rate of absenteeism for something like this is around 80%. And about 20% of attendees are usually only able to stay focused on the subject for three out of every ten minutes. Most are reading 'emails' on their mobiles. That's when they haven't left the room entirely to take an 'urgent call'. But this time it's different. Everyone is there both physically and mentally. The person leading the training session actually seems tired at the end, like they've done something. It's his own fault for engaging in stimulating cerebral activity for such an extended period of time. He's just not used to it anymore.

It's 12.30 pm. Usually by this time I would have run out to buy a sandwich, brought it back to the office and eaten it over the keyboard of my computer without looking at it once. No time to even blink as I devour the words on the screen in front of me. I'd check my emails or surf the web as I chewed on my modest lunch like a vacant machine. I'd nourish my brains with as much information as I possibly could, ignoring my poor stomach's real dietary needs.

But there's no screen to devour now. I wonder what it would be like to have a 'real' lunch. You know, like people used to do in the good old days? Before this electronic revolution that has made life so much faster that it doesn't even leave us the time to properly nourish our own body.

It would surely be a huge victory for the stomach in these times of flatlining brainwaves.

'Hi Victoire. You got plans for lunch?'

'Not really. Actually, with everything going on here, I don't really know what to do with myself. It's like I've got too much time, you know? It's so… weird. We've been so busy these past few months. I guess it's funny. It's not like I have absolutely nothing to do, though. You know what I mean. I have stuff to do but really, it's not a lot, at all.'

'So, you want to go grab a bite with me?'

'Err, yeah, sure, OK. Why not. It'll give us a chance to talk about something other than this. You want to check out that Italian? Would make a change from all those sandwiches and salads!'

When we return to the office, I see that I've received a message from Susie Brown, one of the Brussels attendees based in Sydney. Due to the time difference and problems with communication, she's only just received the message about the meeting being canceled. It turns out that Susie was already in the plane when I sent out the cancelation message and she only listened to my voice message once she had touched down for her connecting flight in San Francisco.

'Angeline, thank you for message. I'm going catch a flight back to Sydney in that case after catching up with a client here in San Francisco. It hasn't been a total waste of time as I managed to do a little shopping at the airport!' In the end it seemed she wasn't too bothered at all by the unfortunate situation.

Martine has taken it upon herself to try and raise everyone's spirits with nice little gestures. In the early afternoon she announces that there'll be cold drinks given out to everyone in the office and that tomorrow we're all invited to lunch for pizza.

People are now starting to hope that our predicament lasts a little while longer. We're torn between wanting to get back to work and having our managers take care of us like this every day. It seems something really is changing.

In the afternoon I start thinking about some new product lines we're launching. I begin to note some ideas on my computer that I've brought from home so I can actually do some work.

To top off this rather lovely day, I receive an invitation in a pristine white envelope to attend a European summit on cybersecurity.

It's now six days since the attack. We're all getting used to hurriedly checking our messages on WhatsApp each morning for some fresh updates on the situation from the famous Gold Team.

Here's today's message:

****

1. We expect emails to come back on line tomorrow by European business opening time.

2. As emails come online everyone with a mobile phone will get an SMS message headed 'Emergency Message' from the +49 657 6876582 to alert them.

3. One of the first emails you receive will be instructions to change your password.

4. You will receive a second email that will explain how we will bring our other services online.

5. We have already begun to restore wi-fi but this needs to be carried out on an office by office basis so please be patient.

6. If you urgently need a document please contact Blaise Faure on +32 654 655325 or Clare Walker on + 44 7654 75446 for Europe queries, Kate Flower in Sydney on +61 654 366 654 for Asia Pacific, Jonathan Wagner on +1 654 370-9876 for North America.

7. Most of our offices have already set up rooms with shared computers. If you have no firm or personal laptop, please contact your office manager.

8. Please continue to refer any media enquiries, without commenting, to Kate Vandevelde on +32 987589591.

We all very much appreciate your patience and forbearance.

Many thanks
Gold Team

****

I've got a niggling feeling that somehow our emails won't be working tomorrow. In any case, like the rest of my colleagues, I'm pretty used to working without them now. They take too much effort anyway. We're getting by just fine. Our incredible practicality has let our ingenuity run free and now we can overcome any kind of challenge.

Seven days since the attack.
Getting by.

Although we're now approaching the middle of the second week without our usual means of communication, nor the vast majority of the tools we need to work, it's important to keep our sense of humor to help us get through the day. Anything that used to take only a few of seconds now takes many, or may even take a few hours.

I'm slowly beginning to remember all of the tasks that were on my 'to-do' list. The very thought of completing them now seems next to impossible. All because of (a lack of?) technology. How am I supposed to send documents, call my colleagues or print something? It's impossible. All I have is a computer that is still very much non-operational and a smartphone.

WhatsApp has very quickly become our go-to method of communication to talk to colleagues on the other side of the world, replacing emails for the time being. That's a done deal.

In terms of hardware, before the crash I had a laptop computer with two big, bright screens to work with. Now, as well as two big black screens, I have:
- two cell phones (personal and professional)
- a tablet
- a laptop (personal)
- a professional laptop, still turned off, having been eaten away, hollowed out and destroyed from the inside by this horrible little pest.

With all of this technology at my disposal, it still isn't easy to get things done.

I finally found out how the directors have been able to communicate with each other. Apparently I need to reactivate an old conference call login from four years ago. It's a number from when we still actually used regular telephones that didn't require the internet to function. Now we think of these things as old pieces of junk that can't even handle multiple callers at the same time. I think we're all pretty happy that they didn't end up in the trash now, though. At some point or another, everyone has to suffer their turn of being called useless. Today, I even learned how to connect to the internet on my laptop using my smartphone as a hotspot.

How are you supposed to work when nothing functions anymore and there's a deadline that can't be postponed? You use whatever tools you have on deck and get it done, that's how. But what tools are there on this barely-floating ship with no navigation equipment?

Take a photo of the document you need to send and attach it to a personal email. Bingo!

Find the numbers of people you need to contact on the company website, which hasn't been affected by the attack. Write them on a piece of paper and call them using your smartphone. It only takes four hours to make ten calls (yes, I've already worked out the average call times post-attack).

Bring your own computer to work and - yes,

it's been done - your own printer.

Go and buy your own computer from a nearby store if needs be. I know people who have done this.

Procrastinate about buying USB keys for as long as possible, and if this purchase puts the financial resources of the company into jeopardy, hesitate even longer so you can take your time deciding what size key you actually need. Engage in an enormously long conversation with the person who has volunteered to go and buy them.

Running out of ideas? You can always clean your desk. The only problem is that I've got nothing else to tidy on mine. There are no papers; everything is on the computer these days. And I could really do with tidying the folders on my PC! No need to do that anymore, though, someone else beat me to it.

In the meantime, I remain just as distraught even though the meeting has been canceled. I have a complete product line plan that I can't share with anyone. I'm temporarily redundant.

I'M SENDING
THE REPORT
BY TEXT!

"JUST GET IT
DONE" IS THE
NEW COMPANY
POLICY!

EternalBlue

EternalBlue, is the name of an exploit (a piece of software developed for malicious purposes) developed by the U.S. National Security Agency that takes advantage of a vulnerability in Windows' Server Message Block, and was used by WannaCry to enter into our system and destroy everything in sight.

Eternal blue.

I love the poetic creativity these computer experts have. Blue is such a beautiful color, loved by many.

Eternal: makes me think of eternal happiness and eternal love.

When the two words are put together, it makes me think of the immense size of the ocean or the sky. It's beautiful. It's calm. It's relaxing.

I'm staring out of my window contemplating the point where the eternity of the sky meets the eternity of the ocean. I get lost in these gentle thoughts, I feel my wanderlust spirit begin to awaken. My boat bobs on the waves, I'm floating up towards the stars. This attack may actually have done some good in the end. It's been years since I've had such a wonderful daydream.

Wait. That's not it, at all. This eternal blue is a gaping hole in Windows that lets software into your network and destroy everything. A giant data-eating beast. I don't know why, but for some reason I imagine the creature to be black or brown in color. Definitely not blue. This is no Smurf! Nor is it one of those things from Avatar. This is a horrible, malevolent thing. I hope that it dies from overeating. The only thing immense about it is the immense amount of pain and destruction it has caused.

I think that these IT experts, whether they're from Microsoft, Apple, the NSA or my own multinational company, all need to go back to the drawing board when it comes to naming these things. I don't think they've fully understood the nuances of the semantics involved. I would have

gone for something more like BlackDevil, BigSlimyMonster or StinkingHole. I think that would have been much better suited to this awful creation that allowed such a terrible beast march uninhibited into our system without so much as an ID check.

Reassuring news, for someone...
Eight days since the attack.

Eight days after the attack, one of the very few members of the IT team actually based in Strasbourg decides to give us an update in our own language. Until this point, everything has been in English, and although we're all able to get by, it's just a lot easier to have something of this nature explained in your mother tongue. This poor guy probably hasn't been sleeping well recently. I guess he's under a lot of pressure, too. It probably explains why his prose isn't of the highest literary standard, more of a 'franglais' that blends technical terms as well as a few that I think he's invented himself. I don't think I've ever read a message from him that I've fully understood, but under the current circumstances, I think I'm willing to make an exception.

****

The latest news:

- E-mails on iOs devices will be disponible around 4 am (Strasbourg time);
- IT is reasonably confiant that this deadline will be respected (please expect to receive un avalanche of emails that have backed up since our servers went down;
- A process will be disponible for those who need urgent access to documents sur Workshare (see my next message);
- Wi-Fi will be back working tomorrow, but... only devices (iPhones and iPads) that were déjà saved to the network will be able to connect to it;
- You can keep using Gmail via your own

computer and connecting avec HotSpot;

- Unaffected PCs will be able to connect from tomorrow (but more likely Friday in my opinion) which anyone can use to access docs sur Workshare;

- Les téléphones should work again Friday;

- Computers that have only been lightly affected by this disease will not be disponible before next week;

- Very big advice: do not turn on laptops that were switched off during the alert.

Voilà for now

Stéphane Bertrand, IT Strasbourg
****

It seems like good news, but I'm still not so sure. Now I'm daydreaming again about this image of an avalanche of emails that's going to arrive as soon as we unclog this hole.

I can just imagine the hundreds of thousands of emails pressed up against the door just waiting for it to be opened. They've been outside waiting in the cold for eight days now. There's a mixed atmosphere of irritation and excitement as they sense they're getting closer to their destination. But the door remains closed. One thing is for sure though, that as soon as that door is opened they will all come flooding in. All of a sudden, everyone will become incredibly busy again as they catch up on what they've missed. We've tried to survive without them, but it's beginning to become impossible. The department in which I work is classed as 'internal', so in fact I'm not really one of the main victims of the so-called incoming avalanche. The large majority of colleagues that I work with also had no way to send or receive emails. So rather than an avalanche, I'm probably going to be faced with nothing more than a light spring drizzle.

*When it's nearly the weekend,
everyone's a bit lost...*

Should we believe what they're telling us this time? Everyone is wondering the same thing on this ninth morning since the attack. It's not the first message we've received telling us that things are going to be back to normal, and then nothing happens. I keep shaking my smartphone in the hope that it will somehow trigger this avalanche. Everyone is anxiously waiting to hear its rumble. I can't wait to have this delightful feeling of being busy and having something to do with my day.

The daily email update from IT falls like a cleaver on the chopping board.

****

News

Although our IT services were unable to get our emails back up and running last night, we can still see some light at the end of the tunnel. I won't give you the exact deadline that has been communicated to me for the emails to be back, but it should be by the end of the day.

There is already limited access to Workshare documents.

Please inform your colleagues and your team not to contact the IT team until there is further news.

Stéphane

****

Later the same day.

****

News about the shared equipment room:
In the Madrid room there are 3 laptops
connected to the Wi-Fi and the printer.
****

Wow, at this rate...

The weekend arrived quicker than I had
expected. We decide during our chat at the coffee
machine (where people are hanging out now more
than ever) that Fridays are essentially pointless and
the weekend really began this morning.

In February 2014, American companies belonging to the leisure group Las Vegas Sands were the victims of a major cyberattack including the pirating of their system, a massive theft of confidential data, and the shutting down of a large proportion of their information and communication network. The attack was attributed to a group of Iranian hackers as a response to the public declaration in October 2014 from billionaire and majority shareholder in Las Vegas Sands, Sheldon Adelson, that he would like to see Tehran razed to the ground in a nuclear fire.

In November and December 2014, Sony Pictures Entertainment becomes the victim of a major leak of data, released piece by piece and claimed by the group 'Guardians of Peace'.

The right to come back in the third week.

They seem to feel they need to tell us each day that things still aren't working. It's now 10 days since the attack and the beginning of the third week, and it appears that all of the temporary measures we've taken to continue working are going to have to become permanent ones.

Our computers have all been labeled over the weekend. It's about time the IT team did something that might appear to help our progress.

They feel ashamed because they weren't able to protect us. And we're trying not to be annoyed with them because, after all, it didn't just happen to us, it also happened to some of the most well protected companies in the world. Fine. But still, it's hard not to think that someone, somewhere at some point didn't do their job as well as they could have. Now they are, sure. Now they're working night and day to fix this. It'll make up for all those years when they looked down on us with despise, sneering at us like idiots who didn't have a clue how a computer really worked, who barely knew how to even open the program to write our useless ramblings.

Now I am rambling. Neither anger nor hate nor bitterness is going to get anyone anywhere. Let's get back to the labels. They informed us (by WhatsApp, obviously) that our computers had been isolated, tested one by one, and, depending on the level of infection, color coded using stickers. The hot topic of conversation among colleagues this morning has of course been 'what color's your ticket?'

The lucky ones get a green ticket. They're clean, uninfected, pure. The only thing for them is that they can't connect to anything. They can be switched on and used, but as if the internet didn't exist. They are alone, not connected to the matrix.

The medium-lucky but not desperate ones got an orange label. They were infected but not seriously compromised. Orange labelers were somewhat relieved but still absolutely forbidden from using their computer for any kind of work at all.

The final category was for those whose only option left was to cry. Plague victims placed into quarantine; banished entirely from the digital playground, they were marked with a red label. They would not be reunited with their machine.

A green label meant that you were not connected to the network at the time of the attack. Maybe you were on vacation, out for a walk or simply not working. The 'oranges' were connected but not actively using their computers at the time (they were in a meeting for example). The 'reds' were on their computers at the exact moment of the attack and were frantically working away as the dirty monster was gobbling up all of their files.

And there of course, as I knew it would be, was a big red sticker on the side of my computer when I arrived this morning.

****

Useful info (received today): if you need a colleague's mobile number, please contact reception on +32 5436 76544. The receptionists have all mobile numbers available.
****

Perfect timing.

The routine

My new and much more tranquil journey to work has become something of a routine. It includes opening up all of my WhatsApp groups and checking for the latest updates on what's happening with the system that refuses to work again.

****

Last message:

Following the information communicated to you this morning, finally e-mails will not become active again today. The IT team is continuing to work hard to find a solution as quickly as possible, and we will let you know of any developments as soon as they happen.

Blah blah blah.

Blah blah blah.

We will be providing more detailed information about the situation once everything is operational. We will let you know as soon as this is the case.

****

I've seen this before. This really is becoming my new routine. And it's the weekend again. Already. Still, we did manage to get some conference calls done with our mobile phones. The Brussels meeting even got rescheduled to October.

Return of the emails.

Julie
'Hey everyone. Je suis très sorry to bother everyone on a Sunday but I really need to know something! Are any of you receiving emails again on your phones? Let me know ASAP! It's urgent.'

Jean-Louis
'I got a message by text giving me a code to use so for my mails, but I haven't tried it yet because I wasn't sure if it was real. The message was from 06 54 32 58 96. Do you know whose number that is, Julie?'

Julie
'Yeah it's OK to use. If the code doesn't work you get a popup.'

Jean-Louis
'OK, thanks. I'll try it.'

Valentine
'You need to go into settings.
That's what I had to do.
I've been receiving my mails since yesterday.
Blackout between Tuesday and Friday.'

Julie
'OK.'

Valentine
'I only got my mails for last Monday until Tuesday afternoon.'

Jean-Louis
'My code didn't work. I'm gonna try again later because I'm out of battery and not at my place.'

Julie
'I'll see tomorrow then. No worries. I'll just say I couldn't get hold of anyone. It's a new day tomorrow! Have a good evening everyone.'

Jean-Louis
'Yeah I just tried again and it didn't work btw.
It says that my info has either changed or isn't correct.'

Julie
'Yeah don't worry about it. I'll figure it out tomorrow dear.'

Jean-Louis
'Sounds good… Have a nice evening.'

Marc
'Julie, I put the code in when I went into settings, and got 2 e-mails from Saturday July 1 (which were not sent originally on the 1st) and one from today from IT helpdesk which is the same as your message above. See you tomorrow anyway!'

Julie
'Thanks, Marc. So you're getting your mails again like me, but it's not the same for everyone. Good news that they're coming back little by little.'

Marc
'At last, a bit of light at the end of the tunnel.'

Vincent
'I got more mails later in the evening, four external work mails and two from IT. Things are improving.'

Back to normality.

It's now four weeks since 'it' happened. Since 'it' entered our system and nearly destroyed everything.

In the end, we all managed to adapt. It's during these moments that you can see that the human being isn't quite as resistant to change as we might sometimes think. Whatever happens, you need to be able to adapt. We found ways to work with what we had and we got on with the job. We did whatever it took to make sure that constant struggle wasn't the new normal.

Sometimes, starting from zero may not be such a bad thing. Before all of this happened, our intranet set up was a total mess. Everyone complained about how poorly designed it was, that you could never find what you wanted in the confused shambles of badly indexed pages. The structure was non-sensical and all of the information it contained, if you were lucky enough to find what you were looking for, was all out of date, obsolete, half complete, old or unusable. Now they really do have something to complain about: there's only one page left. Just one. It's incredibly rudimentary and contains only the most essential information.

Under the current circumstances, here's what is considered 'essential':

- The number of the information hotline, which is so useful at the moment that it has been placed directly in the center of the page. Below that is a list containing the programs and systems that are working again. Meaning not very many. At this stage though a little goes a long way.
- The numbers of certain departments that are considered to be fundamental, such as finance, HR, the internal travel agency and the pitch writers.

That's it.

Since the Brussels meeting was cancelled, I've been struggling to get back into the groove, so to speak. Projects that I was working on before now seem to have a different flavor. It's made me rethink the value of doing certain things that I had been doing before. I no longer see the point of certain parts of my job, now that I have witnessed the infinite fragility of it all and experienced this sense of utter uselessness.

The virus has destroyed the majority of my work. I begin to wonder where the virus is now. Has it been destroyed? Did it self-destruct? Is it hiding somewhere still, with just one little end of it poking out, ready to strike when the coast is clear? No one is answering these questions.

As I look out over the vast workspace, all I can see are ruins. Now it's a case of us all finding the energy to pull up our sleeves and rebuilding it all.

EternalRomance

EternalRomance is the name of another exploit that is able to take advantage of a Windows vulnerability, and is the other possible entry method used by the worm to get into our system.

As if one wasn't enough.

Eternal romance.

It's just further proof of the endless poetic creativity of IT experts. Do they really have nothing better to do than to find poetic names for their mistakes? Their time would be better spent on their actual job: creating systems and applications without vulnerabilities.

Eternal romance. What will they come up with next?

Over the past few days, a lot people have developed a very strong eternal hatred towards the person who developed this beast. If this is romance, I want none of it. It's a little bit of sadomasochistic for a love story. Not my thing.

We're back.
Because life always finds a way.

Today is a very special day. I've never been so happy to go and collect a computer. The one I'm getting will be brand new with an empty hard drive. I'm starting from scratch. It will proudly be carrying a 'Super Green' label. Is it weird that this makes me feel pretty good? It's like I've just done a really good spring clean. A new beginning. Everything is shiny and clean. After everything that has happened recently, it feels great.

There's a lot to rebuild though, and it's going to take an awful lot of work.

I need to re-enter my password every time I do anything now: to get into the thingumajig portal, to print my documents from the cloud, to get into my holiest-of-holies email account and anything else that had been installed and set up over days, months, years. Now it all has to be reinstalled and I need to explain everything again to my computer. All of my passwords have to be changed and each one must be unique and 'uncrackable'. That's not easy to do.

We're all very happy to have the previous conference call system back again that announces the name of each person as they join the group, as well as the waiting time to get into the virtual meeting room. It's a function that might seem useful at first, but actually ends up being a bit of a waste of time when even a just few seconds are precious.

We no longer receive all of the emails from

who-knows-where that we did before. All of those spam messages that polluted our inboxes (and so our lives, in a way) are now filtered out and frankly it's a welcome consequence. The rather intrusive system that used to tell us whether or our colleagues were connected to the network, or whether they were busy somewhere in a meeting, has not be reinstalled. It served nothing other than to help people, myself included I admit, snoop on others. It's given us a new sense of freedom. No more stalking or being stalked. Now no one will be able to tell if I'm connected or not, available or on the telephone, in a meeting or otherwise occupied. And that's just fine by me.

I feel like I'm living in a Back To the Future movie:

- Human resources are now using paper once again to keep track of incoming and outgoing employees.

- To book a meeting room we now need to fill out a form and give it to reception. All request forms are placed in a big green folder. A pencil and paper never let anyone down!

- Regular landline phones are back on our desks.

- All calls must once again go through a switchboard before they are transferred to us, which is a huge waste of time, of course: 'I have Ms. Thingy for you, Mr. Whatsyaname.' I'd forgotten that this type of system had ever existed.

- I now have no idea how to submit my end of year reports, because the system into which I used to enter all of the information has now disappeared into thin air. Will it come back one day? I have to admit that I wouldn't be totally distraught if this one didn't make its way back from the ashes.

- Articles which I had read and found interesting enough to save in case I needed them again one day have all gone. So that was a waste of time, then. I wonder if it's better to just completely change how I do things. Everything of any importance now exists or is saved in some digital form, so perhaps it would be safer for me to let someone else take care of it and just put it all on the mysterious cloud. Especially now that I know it can all be ruined in a split second by one nefarious little worm.

- The IT teams are still talking about things that I don't understand. What exactly is a cache inbox? I just want my emails to work, and even better if they can work exactly as they did before. A cache inbox. It sounds like somewhere you'd put money, although I'm almost certain that's not what I would find there.

Somehow, for reasons that I don't understand, all of my internet bookmarks have been saved from destruction!

In February 2016, the Bangladesh Bank was hacked, losing $81 million in the process.

Another bank, Ecuadorian this time, la Banco del Austro, was also the victim of a cyberattack in 2015. It was only confirmed however on May 22, 2016. The cost to them was €10.7 million.

YUM! YUM!

News from Dominic Invulnerable

Now it's all about getting back to work. And that's not so simple. We all need to admit that in some way we're a little embarrassed by what happened to us. When the issue was discussed in official communiqués, it was referred to not as a 'cyberattack', but rather an 'IT incident', a 'blackout' or an 'interruption'.

Our clients were very understanding. Well, they were for a while. We assured them that none of their data had been leaked. Oh no. They were destroyed. It was the lesser of two evils, really. Nothing got out. Everything was vaporized, the beast devoured it all.

The new normal is a place that looks just like it did before, which is reassuring, but in fact isn't the same at all when you look closely. We got nearly all of our applications back, but not everything. We now know that in the time it takes for lightning to strike, which it did at the end of June, we went from 3,200 applications to 0. That's pretty rapid. They won't remake every one of them, but everyone seems to agree that this is not a bad thing.

We're now a few weeks post-attack, and it still works as a good excuse for why we haven't made as much progress with our work as we should have. But that will only hold out for a while. We all know that.

I've also noticed that our IT team has been conspicuously silent. After the barrage of reassuring messages that we received every day during the crisis, now I get absolutely nothing from our CIO. No emails telling us how everything is going to be OK, that he was going to take care of everything. I don't know if the lack of news is worrying or comforting.

Silence.

Again, silence.

Heads would roll again a few months later:

****

Email from the Big Boss to all the teams
Subject: Changes within the teams

Dear all,
After fifteen years serving our company, Dominic Invulnerable has decided that it is time for

him to take his career in a new direction. To this end, he will be leaving us at the end of the month. As you all know, we've recently been through an extremely difficult period with our IT systems. Thanks to the advice of experts, all of them have been restored to perfect working order. We have used this as an opportunity to rethink our entire IT architecture and build a new system for the future. We are still learning lessons from this experience, which although difficult has made us stronger. I have personally been touched by the solidarity of the teams and your professionalism which has allowed this large company to maintain its activities despite the difficulties.

I wish you all happy holidays,

Martin Onmylittlecloud
Your CEO

****

When I arrived this morning, I saw a man standing in a doorway that is normally always closed. I had zero clue there was anything behind this door. Behind the man I can see a forest of tangled wires and tiny red and green lights flashing. The young man in the doorway looked exasperated as he moved his ladder toward the wiry mess. I don't know what he was intending to do. Was he going to pull them all out and reconnect them? Good luck to him if that's the case, it's like one giant ball that will be a nightmare to untangle.

Seriously, what has been going on here?

The whole story.

On May 12 and 13, 2017, a widescale cyberattack paralyzed the computers of multinational companies and public services in one hundred countries. The cyberattack spread through e-mails containing an internet link which, once clicked, allowed a worm to be downloaded onto the computer. It worked by exploiting the obsolete Windows XP operating system as well as previous versions that hadn't been updated. The virus then delivered a 'payload', comprised of malware, which encrypted the data contained on the computer before demanding a ransom payment in exchange for a key to decode the files. The number of computers affected by the virus is estimated to be up to 230,000, in 150 different countries.

On June 27, 2017, a massive new wave of global cyberattacks, the mode of operation of which was 'reminiscent of the WannaCry attacks suffered on May 12 and 13, 2017' affected hundreds of thousands of computers all over the world. The first computers began to show symptoms of infection at around 11 am that morning, the first signs in France were around four hours later.

The attack struck major companies in the Ukraine first, affecting the operations of their banks and airports. In Russia, petroleum giant Rosneft was targeted, as well as large banks, Ukranian government structures, Mars, Nivea and retail giant Auchan. Information from the screens of the computers indicated that the worm 'demanded a ransom of $300'. On its Facebook *page, the Kiev metro indicated that it 'cannot accept payments by bank card at its ticket office due to a cyberattack.' There were flight delays at Kiev airport due to signage problems. Over the next few hours, the attacks became larger in scale until the situation was described as a 'global cyberattack', affecting a large number of multinational companies.*

The ransomware (that has since been named NotPetya) would be displayed instead of the Windows logo each time a computer was restarted. A message written in red over a black background stated, in English:
'Ooops, your important files are encrypted. If you see this text, then your files are no longer accessible, because they have been encrypted. Perhaps you are busy looking for a way to recover your files, but don't waste your time. Nobody can recover your files without our decryption service.'

The ransom was to be paid in $300 worth of Bitcoin, which, once paid, would give the user access to their files again. Many of the files were in fact destroyed rather than encrypted. Computer security expert Matt Suiche affirms that the message served nothing other than to feed the media machine and that the real objective of the attack was sabotage. According to his analysis, no data survived the attack, it was simply replaced with something else. Hard disks were in all cases irredeemable.

Unlike the WannaCry attack, there was no way of stopping NotPetya from spreading via a 'kill switch', nor a way to unencrypt your files once they had been compromised. The ransomware installed itself via automatic updates or an executable file (.exe). The virus would cause the computer to restart and then the infamous 'blue screen of death' would be displayed before the Windows hard disk error checking tool would perform a fake check and the ransom demand appeared.

Once the virus had its foot in the door by landing on a computer within a larger network, NotPetya would commence spreading to the other machines in the networks. The malware had a couple of cunning ways to do this. It contained two pirating tools stolen from the NSA, namely EternalBlue and EternalRomance, the exploits that Microsoft had issued a patch for a few months previously but that some machines had not installed or they were still running old versions of Windows that contained the exploit.

If it couldn't gain entry using either of these methods, the malware would search for the passwords of the computer's administrator and, if possible, use it to connect to other terminals in the network. If it found a server, it would deposit an executable file (.exe) which would then be activated remotely using Microsoft's remote administration tool. This allowed the hackers to even infect computers that had the latest security updates. If the company's network is connected to another external network, there is nothing to stop the virus from spreading to another organization.

Just like WannaCry, NotPetya targeted companies and organizations. But unlike its predecessor, it didn't spread 'in the wild' via the internet. According Microsoft, the first infection occurred in the Ukraine: the hackers utilized an update to a piece of Ukrainian accounting software named MEDoc in order to infiltrate their malevolent code onto the network of a local company. Another infection vector of the NotPetya ransomware was identified: the website of the Ukrainian city of Bakhmut, in Donetsk Oblast. The hackers managed to lay a trap on the city's homepage in the form of a fake Microsoft Windows update.

After the Great Game massacre...

First of all, let's take a moment to think about all of the attacks that we haven't heard about. The ones that didn't get such attention. It's a shame, because they could have really made us laugh. Like the one that affected the food distribution network and changed the weighing software for fruits and vegetables. You'd get to the counter with a big bunch of bananas and discover that they cost the same as one grape. In fact, that was just a practice run by a large retailer to prepare for such a situation, should it ever occur. Then there was the cat litter tray that had its price changed to that of an expensive bottle of vintage Bordeaux, and the food mixer whose price was reduced to a carton of yoghurt. One can only imagine that chaos that will happen once these systems are all truly interconnected.

While we're imagining such a scenario, what else could hackers have in store for us in the future? Maybe they'll...

- Switch passenger flight details: you think you're going to San Diego, but end up in Mumbai.
- Have your boss' salary paid into your bank account and yours into theirs. As well as helping you out with your finances, it also has farther reaching benefits: your boss, whose interest in the subject of your finances right now is close to absolute zero, would suddenly become aware of the gaping disparity of your situation and theirs.
- Mess up store loyalty schemes by giving you 100% discounts on all of your favorite products.
- Make everyone who has a ticket a part-

winner on the lottery. Like the French TV show L'École des fans, in which it didn't matter who won the singing contest, because the host would eventually declare every child a winner. It would also be sweet revenge for all the lottery commercials over the years telling us how everyone wins.

- Pay off all of your loans at the bank and give you a nice bonus with lots of zeros on the end.

- Connect your bank card to the account of someone else. Every time you buy something, it's someone else who pays. It's better than the inverse.

- Have your retirement savings company mail you telling you that you've saved enough to leave your job and live the good life from here on in.

These types of attacks are fine to imagine and laugh at, but it's good remind ourselves that we are living in a time when we should be prepared for disruptions to occur to our daily lives because of this relatively new type of threat. Here are a few more attacks that have (seriously) happened recently:

- Over a period of almost six months, a prestigious auditing and consultancy firm was the victim of a huge cyberattack during which hackers gained access to private information, such as email exchanges between the firm and its clients. They used the username and password of an administrator to enter the system as well as access a platform containing significant amounts of confidential data.

- A famous American credit card company that supposedly specialized in data protection was the victim of a large cyberattack in 2017. The data of over 140 million Americans and over 200,000 bank card numbers were stolen by the hackers, who exploited a vulnerability in one of the company's systems, giving them access to protected files. A few days after the attack, the CEO announced that he would be resigning from his position.

- A well-known streaming service was hit by a huge pirating attack that involved spamming its users. Millions of them received emails asking for them to hand over their bank details if they didn't want their account to be closed. As always, everything had been carefully designed to trick the users into believing the mail was authentic, including a link to a website that used the exact graphics chart of the real platform, replicating it down to the very last detail.

- The ransomware DoubleLocker attacked not computers, but mobile phones. For the first time ever, ransomware was able to change a user's PIN and encrypt the data contained on a phone or tablet. Having no other way of accessing their phone's data, victims of the attack were forced to pay the ransom demanded by the hackers.

- An attack on an image sharing platform that took place in 2014 was not discovered until 2017. Almost 1.7 million users were victims of the attack which threatened to unveil their personal data, including email addresses and passwords. With more than 150 million users worldwide, the platform asked all of its users to immediately change their passwords, and to do the same for other platforms owned by the same company.

- Almost 57 million user accounts for Uber were hacked as part of an enormous data breach in 2016. The American company paid the hackers $100,000 in exchange for the destruction of the stolen data, even though they had no real way of knowing that the hackers would hold up their end of the bargain.

- A piece of malware named Reaper used a method that was not new to the malware genre, but was executed on an unprecedented scale. Over one million organizations were scanned looking for connected objects that were badly protected.

What do we really know about all of this software that we install on our devices? These programs and applications that observe (spy on?) us and remember everything that we've done?

What has been presented in this book

should be enough to cause a general panic. If not a panic, then just enough to cause us all to laugh at the fragility of our new world; a world that believes itself to be so very tough and resilient. Or perhaps it will just serve as a reminder that we must always learn from our mistakes.

So, what can we conclude from all of this?

As we enter into this period of Cyber Warfare, it is of vital importance that we return to the fundamental things in life, at work and in our private lives. In this virtual world, this experience has taught me something. Or at least it has shown me something that deep down I had been aware of for many years: that this world is fragile, including the world of technology and communication that has changed our lives so profoundly over the past few years. Let's remember that all we are talking about is a sequence of 0s and 1s and that something so trivial should not have such an effect on our lives.

I'm sat in my garden on this beautiful June evening, almost exactly one year to the day after the events described within this book took place.

The rooster has just sung his cock-a-doodle-do to inform the entire neighborhood (which is basically made up of some squirrels, turtledoves, frogs, forest birds and other chirpy things) that he's doing just fine with his three chick friends. On top of the chicken coop by the hedge, he reigns over his domain.

The birds are singing to bring the sunset. The turtledoves are cooing as the night approaches.

The little chicks born only a few days ago in the nest on the roof of my house are chirping, calling their parents who are flying relentlessly back and forth in the last rays of sun to feed them.

The mosquitoes are out in full force after the rather tropical spring this year.

Nature is all connected, and I am connected to nature. That's what really matters.

193

Acknowledgments

To all of my colleagues who also lived through this experience with me.

To Folco Chevallier for his support and precious advice via the BookLeaders Academy.

To Cécile, Isabelle, Christophe, Christine, Patrice, my proofreaders from the beginning.

To the animals in the forest.

To Pépito, Granola, Myrtille and Groseille for their purrs of encouragement.

To the associates of Effective Yellow, the creator of the Effective Pilot program, Frédéric Vilanova and Christophe Clarinard for their confidence. They have been enthusiastic promoters of the messages in this book since FIC 2019.

<u>From the same author</u>

Global Work: it's a topsy-turvy world! –
@GlobalWork Collection - Part I
Text by Angeline Vagabulle, Illustrations by
Renard, English translation by Andrew Baggaley, in
e-book or print.

1. Leave your review for 'Cyberattack' on Amazon.
It only takes a few minutes and helps the
community of people who won't look at their inbox
or their colleagues in the same way again to grow!

2. Follow the latest news about the
@GlobalWorkCollection on Facebook, LinkedIn,
Twitter (@vagabulle), Instagram or my website.

http://angelinevagabulle.wixsite.com/angelinevagabulle

Thalia NeoMedia / DG Éditions Les Funambulles

First printed: October 2019

ISBN : 978-2-491222-02-4